Learning to Speak a New Tongue

Learning to Speak a New Tongue

*Imagining a Way That Holds People Together—
An Asian American Conversation*

FUMITAKA MATSUOKA

◆PICKWICK *Publications* • Eugene, Oregon

LEARNING TO SPEAK A NEW TONGUE
Imagining a Way That Holds People Together—An Asian American Conversation

Copyright © 2011 Fumitaka Matsuoka. All rights reserved. Except for brief quotations in critical publications or reviews, no part of this book may be reproduced in any manner without prior written permission from the publisher. Write: Permissions, Wipf and Stock Publishers, 199 W. 8th Ave., Suite 3, Eugene, OR 97401.

Pickwick Publications
An Imprint of Wipf and Stock Publishers
199 W. 8th Ave., Suite 3
Eugene, OR 97401

www.wipfandstock.com

ISBN 13: 978-1-60899-828-9

Cataloging-in-Publication data:
Matsuoka, Fumitaka

    Learning to speak a new tongue: imagining a way that holds people together—an Asian American conversation / Fumitaka Matsuoka.

    p. ; cm. —Includes bibliographical references.

    ISBN 13: 978-1-60899-828-9

    1. Group identity—United States. 2. Cultural pluralism—United States. 3. Asian Americans—Ethnic identity. I. Title.

E184 A1 M295 2011

Manufactured in the U.S.A.

To Sharon and Emma

Contents

Acknowledgments / ix
Abbreviations / xi

Introduction: What Holds People Together in a Wounded World? / 1

1 The Original Language of American Peoplehood and Its Corruption / 16
2 People On the Way: Translocal and Rupturally Liminal Experience of Race / 25
3 The Spirit of Dissonance and Dissent / 64
4 Amphibolous Faith: Reality Is Multiple / 94
  Conclusion / 126

Bibliography / 137

Acknowledgments

THIS WORK IS A culmination of my listening to the voices of Asian Americans in the last thirty some years. The number of voices has multiplied significantly during these years. My listening began in the small one-room office of Pacific and Asian American Center for Theology and Strategies (PACTS) at Pacific School of Religion (PSR). Then it spread into the gatherings of Asian American church leaders and theologians that were sponsored by then the Fund for Theological Education under the leadership of Dr. Oscar McLoud. The establishment of the Institute for Leadership Development and the Study of Pacific and Asian North American Religion (PANA Institute) in PSR expanded tenfold the arenas of conversation among Asian and Pacific Americans. Nearly coincided with the establishment of PANA Institute was the beginning of Asian Pacific Americans Religions Research Initiative (APARRI), a place of conversation and sharing of research findings among Asian American and Pacific Islander American scholars and graduate students of religion, first began at University of California at Santa Barbara and later administered by PANA Institute. Some of the leaders of APARRI were also members of periodic gatherings of graduate students of UC Berkeley and Graduate Theological Union at Townsend Hall of UCB campus. Asian North American Religion, Culture and Society group of the American Academy of Religion also greatly contributed to the shaping of Asian and Pacific American study of religion and theology. These series of conversation have been, to quote Huston Smith, "like rivers, dynamic and changing, bearing the heritage of the past to water the fields of the present. These rivers are converging and we need to build bridges."

Acknowledgments

I am indebted to countless number of colleagues and students for the publication of this work. I would like to express my deep gratitude to these folks whose names are too many to be mentioned here. I do need to acknowledge the tireless work of critiquing and editing this work done by Dr. Matthew Haar Farris of Dominican University of California at San Rafael, CA. Without his helpful comments this work could not have been completed.

Abbreviations

AJ	*Amerasia Jounral*
AJT	*Asian Journal of Theology*
CC	*The Christian Century*
J JAAC	*Journal of Asian American Cultural Criticism.*
JAAR	*The Journal for the American Academy of Religion*
RPL	*Religion & Public Life*
SLR	*Stanford Law Review*

Introduction

What Holds People Together In a Wounded World?

THE HEART OF THE matter is the search for a new architecture of peoplehood at home and building a new set of relationships abroad for Americans. The question is this: what holds people together as Americans in a world that is increasingly interconnected, yet also fragmented, and wounded? Historically, Americans have believed that democratic freedom—the Bill of Rights, a free economic order, and the security of property—is what holds this nation together. But, this cherished American public religion of democratic freedom and its accompanying civic values are coming under close scrutiny. The scrutiny is being carried out amidst an ever-widening gap between the poor and the super wealthy, and in the increasingly globalized religious, ideological, and political conflicts, and wars that have exposed the conflicting ways of understanding the meaning of life-together. Americans' deeply held values, our "first language" as sociologist Robert Bellah characterizes them, intersect with our political system, religion, race, ethnicity, class, gender, and sexuality.[1] Moreover, the American public religion of democracy is closely associated with wielding its political powers both at home and abroad. Americans are once again reminded that civic values and power are inseparable. Religion—even what is increasingly referred to as "public religion," a sort of secular religion in its own right—is politicized, racialized, and closely associated with power distribution. This is particularly the case for the American public religion of democratic freedom with its distinct deistic Christian origin.

1. Bellah, *Habits of the Heart*.

In recent years Americans are being accused of an "imperialism" and "positional superiority" in our political, economic, cultural, and religious orientations as we relate with our world neighbors.[2] In the wake of 9/11 George Semaan, editor of the London-based Arabic language newspaper, *Al Hayat*, commented that America needs to "change its perspective on how it builds its interests and how it defends them by building a network of relationships that takes into consideration the interests of others who are weak and who have rights but are incapable of imposing these interests or these rights."[3] This book is an attempt to respond to George Semaan's challenge to Americans through a particular lens shaped within the epistemological framework of Americans of Asian descent. The central thesis of this work is that speaking a "second language" learned by Asian Americans within their threefold epistemological scaffold of translocality of race, a particular sensitivity to pathos in the spirit of dissonance and dissent, and an "amphibolous" or hybrid faith, may well provide a clue to building an alternate architectural paradigm of peoplehood. The voices spoken in the second language may also help respond to Semaan's challenge for building a new peoplehood and to redefine democratic freedom as the historical paradigm of American nationhood. A "second language" is a way of speaking of America that grows out of an alternate "storied site," in the site shaped by the language, communal values, and perspective in a particular community of often disfranchised people, where lost memories are recovered, buried histories are retraced, silence emerges in an articulated fashion, and fractured relationships with other disfranchised neighbors are reestablished. A "second language" is the "language of tradition and commitment in a community of memory" to paraphrase the expression of Bellah.[4] A "second language" speaks of our common destiny as Americans and as world citizens, a destiny that is being more pronounced and imperiled at precisely the time when our divisions are deepest.

---

2. bin Talal, "Seeing Iraq's Future By Looking at Its Past."

3. Semaan, *Christian Century*.

4. Bellah names "second languages" to mean "the languages of tradition and commitment in communities of memories. . .that most Americans know as well, and which they use when the language of the radically separate self does not seem adequate." *Habits of the Heart.*, 154. The term "Peoplehood" is chosen instead of the familiar term "nationhood" to indicate an alternate expression of how Americans come together. It is a critique of an increasingly obsolete notion of "nationhood."

A recent event in our nation's capital illustrates the challenge facing America of what holds people together both at home and abroad. In his second term President Bush appointed his longtime confidant Karen Hughes as undersecretary of state for public diplomacy and public affairs. During her Senate confirmation hearings, she told the Foreign Relations Committee, "We are involved in a generational and global struggle of ideas. I recognize the job ahead [to spread democracy and freedom throughout the world] will be difficult. Perceptions do not change easily or quickly."[5] Political analyst David Rieff questioned Hughes' reading of the current hostility directed toward the U.S. in the international scene: "Refreshing though it was for its candor, Hughes' statement neglected the larger question: Is hostility toward the United States based largely on misperceptions of America's actions and intentions or on a genuine dislike of the power America wields around the world?"[6] Believing that a sizeable group of Americans agree that the traditional American ideals should prevail only if these ideals are communicated well enough, Rieff went on to say: "To believe this, however, you must believe that there is an inevitable progress in history—a progress toward freedom."[7] This basic assumption of an inevitable progress toward democracy and freedom in history that is behind U.S. foreign policy is becoming increasingly questionable in today's world both within the U.S. and abroad. At the same time, the view that the role of the U.S. in the world is to spread democratic freedom and the belief in the global application of progress toward freedom does not belong only to the conservative wing of current American politics. It is indeed deeply ingrained in the American psyche, shaped from the foundation of the nation and tempered by the ways American societal coherence, peoplehood, is maintained. This belief in the progress toward democratic freedom has been reinforced particularly in time of war, historically and currently. This is the case in the post 9/11 era with the increasing fear of a violent attack against the U.S. by political and religious extremists. An uncritical belief in the universal application of American democratic freedom is to lose sight of the point of concurrence between the national and the international common good.

---

5. Rieff, "Their Hearts And Minds?" 11.
6. Ibid.
7. Ibid.

Democratic freedom is the foundation of our society, rooted in our collective history, continues to be affirmed and reaffirmed in every critical turn of events in our nation, and is the language we have spoken for so long. It gives rise to the questions that frame this particular work: Is the belief in democratic freedom indeed still a realistic and viable principle for the cultivation of societal coherence of peoplehood for us Americans and for our relationship with our world neighbors? Will this belief contribute to global peace and justice in a world increasingly suspicious of and hostile toward the way the U.S. wields its power? Are there alternate angles of vision, "languages," or life orientations that would meet the challenges of peace and justice more adequately than the historically shaped American ideal of democratic freedom alone in this highly interrelated and yet fragmented and conflicted global life in which we Americans find ourselves today? Or, can America continue to uphold its own democratic principles and values but also temper them in such a way that takes into consideration the wellbeing of its neighbors at home and abroad?

A clue to adequately respond to Semaan's challenge lies, in part, in the use of a "second language" spoken in America. In this work, we will pay attention to the second language spoken by Americans of Asian descent. A "second language," a language of tradition and commitment in a community of memory, is a hybrid language, nuanced and sometimes unfaithful to the official language of the land in which one lives.[8] It is also a language of empathy and compassion, a language learned out of the matrix of "contradicting" experiences of being an American of Asian descent in an officially claimed nation of democracy. A "second language" is a way of speaking of America from the vantage point of an alternate "storied site" where, contrary to the officially prescribed story of America, lost histories and memories are retraced, retrieved, and broken relationships with other disfranchised neighbors are rehabilitated. A "second language" speaks of our common destiny as Americans and as world citizens, a destiny that is being pronounced and imperiled precisely at a time when our divisions are deepest. To begin this exploration into an alternate vision of peoplehood through the lens shaped by the "second language" of Asian Americans, an analysis of its epistemological scaffold is first needed. The term "peoplehood" means more than "nationhood." In fact, "peoplehood" implicitly critiques the historically

---

8. A representative articulation of a "second tongue" is Cha's *Dictee*.

defined parochial and sometimes jingoistic term "nationhood." The basic notion of "peoplehood" is simply that which brings people together. It is the consciousness and values that lie at the foundation of people coming together. "Nationhood" is a provisional form of "peoplehood."

Our particular interpretation of peoplehood has its referential sources both in the "river" of a myriad of representative historical interpretations on the one hand and on the other hand a particular epistemological locus in which the interpreter is situated, a locus from which the distinctness of Asian Americans' shared story is analyzed. In this introductory chapter, a brief description of the scaffold is given. In subsequent chapters each pillar of the scaffold will be analyzed in depth. The scaffold is threefold: 1) the translocal and "rupturally liminal" life embedded in a racialized community resulting in a particular set of value orientations; 3) a diasporic identity that is dissonant with the prevailing societal norms fostering a heightened sensitivity toward pathos in life; and 3) a faith orientation that is an "amphibolous" or hybrid negotiation among myriad faith traditions and cosmologies. These three pillars constitute Asian American epistemology and are critical in analyzing Asian American experiences. These epistemological pillars also shape the contour of this interpretation of peoplehood.

The first pillar of the epistemological scaffold is the meaning of race experienced by Asian Americans. Race points to a translocal life for Asian Americans, full of unpredictable surprises and instability. Historically, Asian immigrants to the U.S. have played critical roles in building the society. Yet "multicultural" America was also predicated on the Orientalist construction of society in which certain groups of immigrants are viewed and treated as foreign in origin and nature.[9] Because of the conflicting and contradicting perceptions of Asian Americans by the broader American society—a "model minority" on the one hand and a "foreigner-within" on the other—we Asian Americans have regarded our racial identity as translocal, not finding a stable place of identity. This translocal racial identity produces cultural and religious expressions in response to the prevailing norm of America as a nation that domesticates and assimilates its diverse inhabitants into a relatively homogeneous society. Thus, translocality is the cultural and religious locus of navigating the conflicting and contradicting treatments of Asian

---

9. For a fuller treatment of this contradicting role of Asian Americans, see Lowe, *Immigrant Acts*.

Americans by America and our own fluid and unstable understanding of identity. In other words, Asian Americans are often not at home in their own homes, displaced within the very society in which they live. This translocal racial identity of Asian Americans has produced a particular cultural and religious value orientation, an alternative site where Lisa Lowe says the "palimpsest of lost memories is reinvented, histories are fractured and retraced, and the unlike varieties of silence emerge into articulacy."[10] This creates a distinct translocal value orientation akin to what Theodor Adorno calls an exilic morality.[11] The conflicting and contradictory racial configuration of Asian Americans makes the condition of having a home impossible; it is "part of morality," then, to recognize how this racial configuration of Asian Americans also excludes others from the condition of being at home in America as well. It is vital to note here that the impact of the way race is constructed for Asian Americans simultaneously affects both those who are the object of the configuration as well as those who initiate the configuration. In the case of Palestine/Israel, this insight may be deployed to suggest that no one, neither Palestinian nor Israeli, can truly be "at home" in the region so long as the structure that generates homelessness is perpetuated. Within the American racial architecture, the contradictory and translocal life orientation of Asian Americans is thus not exclusive to Asian American communities. It affects equally the rest of racialized America. Race is like an enormous spider web: if one touches it anywhere, that touching sets the whole thing trembling.

For Adorno, the impossibility of dwelling securely at home leads one to look to the text, to literary production, for new dwelling. "In his text, the writer sets up house," he suggests.[12] "For a man who no longer has a homeland, writing becomes a place to live." However, text provides only elusive comfort. Adorno notes that, "In the end, the writer is not even allowed to live in his writing."[13] Text provides "at most a provisional

---

10. Ibid., 6.

11. Adorno, *Minima Moralia*, 38–39. Quoted in Said, Reflections on Exile, 564–565. "Dwelling, in the proper sense, is now impossible. The traditional residences we grew up in have grown intolerable: each trait of comfort in them is paid for with a betrayal of knowledge, each vestige of shelter with the musty pact of family interests . . . . The house is past . . . it is part of morality not to be at home in one's home." (quoted in Said, "Reflections on Exile," 564–65).

12. Adorno, *Minima Moralia*, 87.

13. Ibid.

satisfaction, which is quickly ambushed by doubt, and a need to rewrite and redo that renders the text uninhabitable."[14] In a similar fashion, the collectively owned text about American citizenship, the Constitution of the United States, though written before the time of the arrival of Americans of Asian descent, provides "only elusive comfort" and often is "uninhabitable" in Asian Americans' translocal racial experiences. It provides at most a provisional satisfaction, which is quickly ambushed by doubt, and a need to rewrite and redo that renders the text uninhabitable. In other words, Asian Americans live in "the contradictions of Asian immigration, which at different moments in the last century and a half of Asian entry into the United States have placed Asians 'within' the U.S. nation-state, its workplaces, and its markets, yet linguistically, culturally, and racially marked Asians as 'foreign' and 'outside' the national polity," says Lisa Lowe.[15]

The contradictions of Asian American immigration extend, furthermore, to our own understanding of our cultural and religious identities. Asian Americans' race experiences have been ruptural, that is to say, suddenly breakable without a prior warning sign and caused by outside pressures. Rupturally Japanese Americans were horded off to concentration camps even as full-fledged citizens during World War II. Asian Americans' race experiences are also liminal because of the racial, cultural, and religious in-between state in which we find ourselves. Asian Americans liminally negotiate between what we claim to be distinct about us on the one hand and perceptions of all sorts imposed upon us from outside on the other. Such a negotiation also results in ambivalent cultural and racial identity, again not having a stable norm to chart the course of our identity. Rather than conforming to a conventional model of racial identity in which particular racial characteristics are passed on from one generation to another, Asian Americans have been attempting to understand our racial identity in multiple and fluid ways. Thus, the "continuing material contradictions" as Lisa Lowe explains the nature of race are the locus where Asian American collective identities and values are forged and claimed just as much as the locus for the emergence of its distinct value orientation. What emerges out of such a condition, ruptural liminality, is a particular kind of value orientation or positioning, nomadic values and perspecive. When life is translocal, rupturally

14. Said, "Reflections on Exile," 568.
15. Lowe, *Immigrant Acts*, 8.

liminal, and fluid, what is valued is the trust, intimacy, and honesty that arise out of relationship-building and even an unexpected encounter with another person. Stability, security, and insurance, on the other hand, are not as much of a value because they can be taken away anytime. Translocality and ruptural liminality cross borders, breaks barriers of thought and experience. Translocality is a "life led outside habitual order." Such a life "is nomadic," "decentered, contrapuntal," and constantly subject to new disruptions.[16] Translocality and ruptural liminality are an image that depends not on power, but on motion, on daring to go into different worlds, uses a different language and understands a multiplicity of disguises, masks, and rhetoric. A translocal and rupturally liminal person must suspend the claim of customary routine in order to live in new rhythms and rituals, to cross over, traverse territory, and abandon fixed positions all the time. Movement and openness to the future are also valued in contrast to a singular locality, safety, and defensiveness. Race as translocal and rupturally liminal site points to this kind of nomadic value orientation. We realize that our translocal and liminal racial identity is fragile and its transmission to subsequent generations is by no means guaranteed. But our translocal racial experiences say to us that race is a site not only for an alternate value orientation, the morality of "not being at home in one's own home," as much as the locus of a rupturally liminal cultural and religious identity. Race, in other words, is a site to create a new set of conventions, a second language, for interpreting "the reality [Asian Americans] share within the majority through the institutions it creates or infiltrates."[17]

The second pillar of the threefold epistemological scaffold is a culture of dissonance. Asian American culture is dissonant and irresolute within the prevailing societal and cultural milieu. Language as an indispensable means of expressing culture reveals both dissonance and irresolution for Asian Americans. Frantz Fanon notes that "To speak means to be in a position to use a certain syntax, to grasp the morphology of this or that language, but it means above all to assume a culture, to support the weight of a civilization."[18] In a translocal and rupturally liminal life in which one feels displaced and in-between, "local cultural originality" is difficult to achieve. In finding oneself "face to face with the

16. Said, "Reflections on Exile," 357–68.
17. Ibid.
18. Fanon, *Black Skin, White Masks*, 17–18.

language of the civilizing nation" an emerging original culture generates deviation and dissonance from the normative culture.[19] In such a setting, at the same time, deviation and dissonance are expressed in terms of dis-identification, infidelity, and, particularly, dissenting a given normative culture. The language of dissonance and dissent is prevalent in Asian American literature. In Theresa Hak Kyung Cha's Dictee, for example, this language of dissonance and dissent is clearly expressive. The subject of the book writes poorly, stutters, stops, and leaves verbs un-conjugated. She adulterates the Catholic catechism by mocking the expression in it that human beings are created in "God's likeness" as duplication, counterfeiting, carbon copy, and mirroring.

The language of dissonance and dissent points to yet another, deeper epistemological significance for Asian Americans: the emergence of a distinct angle of vision with sensitivity toward pathos in life arising out of a dissonant culture. Carlos Bulosan ,captures this sensitivity: "Why was America so kind and yet so cruel? Was there no way to simplifying things in this continent so that suffering would be minimized? Was there no common denominator on which we could all meet? I was angry and confused and wondered if I would ever understand this paradox."[20] The publicly owned ideal of a democratic nation and the experience of suffering, sorrow, and exclusion from the ideal—captured so well by Bulosan and represented many times over by the narratives of other Asian immigrants—is what America really is. "We are America!," without any resolution or reconciliation between the ideal and the contradicting reality experienced by Asian immigrants, is the wellspring of the sensitivity to pathos that is deeply ingrained in Asia America.

The movement of the spirit of dissent out of dissonance is ritualized and traditionalized into a reliable cultural reference point within the community. Sacrality is, above all, a category of emplacement says scholar of religion Jonathan Z. Smith. The "palimpsest, " as Lisa Lowe terms, of Asian American language of dissonance and dissent is located in a "storied place," a special location that directs attention to our Asian American history where lost memories are reinvented, where the unlike varieties of silence emerge into spoken words connecting intergenerationally through the past of the living and the dead into the present in community. In other words, a representative storied place such as

19. Ibid., 18.
20. Bulosan, *America Is in the Heart*, 147.

the immigration station barracks museum of Angel Island in the San Francisco Bay, the site of Japanese American internment camps during World War II, such as Manzanar and Tule Lake, California, are sacred spaces where "that which is rejected is ploughed back for a renewal of life."[21] In the words of Asian American theologian Joanne Doi, through pilgrimage to these storied sites the "process of history and memory strives to recognize the collective similarities amidst the historical discontinuities and differences, to retrieve recollections as well as challenge the surviving memories and the dominant politics of memory or rather, 'forgetting.'"[22] Thus, the spirit of dissonance and dissent of Asian Americans, collectively as well as individually, moves in ritual such as a pilgrimage to a storied site.

Asian Americans' translocal and rupturally liminal racial identity leads to our conscious positioning in society. This positioning is a willfully dissenting attempt against the officially prescribed history of America. This positioning emerges out of our particular angle of vision forged by the historical disruptions, pain, and dissonance that await excavation and retrieval from within us and in our history. Ritualized acts of excavation and retrieval of these referential points in our personal and collective history are indeed dissenting acts that serve as the glue that binds us together as a community. Our historical injuries and experiences of dissonance carry the memory of a rehabilitative meaning both in regard to Asian Americans ourselves and also in regard to those who have undergone a similar experience of dislocation and dissonance from the prevailing societal norms. These experiences uncover "hidden histories" that fuel the emergence of important social movements of the time. In this sense, the spirit of dissent born out of our dissonance with the dominant racial and cultural groups is both equally subversive and constructive. The spirit of willful dissent is a powerful driving force to move Asian American communities toward the future as educator David Ng calls "People On the Way" and acts as the seedbed for an alternate set of sacred conventions, a bond, and a second language, that brings people together.[23]

The third pillar of the epistemological scaffold from which a second language for Asian Americans emerges is "amphibolous" faith.

21. Douglas, *Purity and Danger*, 162.
22. Doi, "Tule Lake Pilgrimage," 47. Also see Doi, "Bridge to Compassion."
23. Ng, *People on the Way*.

What is an "amphibolus" faith? For Asian Americans, faith is likely to be expressed in a domain of myriad conflicting historical religious traditions such as Buddhism, Confucianism, Hinduism, coming together, forcing us to live in a state of disidentification with any existing religious tradition in which we find ourselves. Furthermore, disidentification is just as material as "religious" in nature; it is the material side of life that informs the disidentification in the religious realm. Translocal and rupturally liminal experience of race and cultural dissonance both inform this religious disidentification. Disidentification expresses a space in which alienation in the cultural, political, and economic domains can be rearticulated spiritually. An "amphibolous faith" is akin to the term aporia as defined by Jacques Derrida. For him, the term aporia refers to a logical contradiction and therefore a "difficulty in choosing" among a myriad of options, "doubt," or, more precisely, a set of blockage, "no road" in the context of the meaning of justice.[24][2] In such a setting, one learns to live with unresolved contradictions even amidst discomfort of irresolution. In the realm of faith, historically theistic religious traditions and non-theistic traditions co-exist in one's being. An Asian American lives a life of "Buddhist Christian," though such a designation may seem contradictory. Nontheistic Buddhism and monotheistic Christianity is "amphibolously" present in an Asian American. Amphibolous faith entails for Asian Americans an interminable experience like the experience of the "undecidable," a "blind spot" (Derrida) in both metaphysics and religion. Polytheistic religious traditions can also co-exist with monotheistic or nontheistic traditions in Asia America. This domain of contradictions becomes particularly acute for Asian American Christians who are simply assumed to embrace the monotheistic claims of the historical Christian faith and, at the same time, are inclined to live with nontheistic cosmologies embedded in the Asian religious traditions we inherit.

---

24. Derrida, "Forces of Law," 24–26. Here Derrida treats the history of justice. He stresses the Greek etymology of the word "horizon": "As its Greek name suggests, a horizon is both the opening and limit that defines an infinite progress or a period of waiting." Justice, however, even though it is un-presentable, does not wait. A just decision is always required immediately. It cannot furnish itself with unlimited knowledge. The moment of decision itself remains a finite moment of urgency and precipitation. The instant of decision is then the moment of madness, acting in the night of non-knowledge and non-rule. Applied in the notion of amphibolous spirituality, there is the "ghost of the undecidable" is always present in amphiboly.

Our faith orientation is likely to be irresolute, "undecidable," and "amphibolous," often forcing us to negotiate among what seems to be the totalizing claims of the monotheistic Christian tradition on the one hand and the deep spiritual and cultural DNA we inherit from our Asian past on the other, but without resolution or decision. The amphibolous life of faith for Asian American Christian translocal people, in particular, is located in the fissure between the exclusive claims of Abrahamic faith orientations and complementary, inclusive Asian cosmological worldviews. An amphibolous faith cannot be reconciled into a neatly formulated creed or any other form of clear articulation. We just live with amphibology, a grammar that defies a strictly or straightforwardly logical articulation. Furthermore, amphibology "disorients" any conventional spiritual practice, .since it defies not only conventional religious paradigms but also lives in an asymmetrical domain caught between the dominant religious paradigm and the multiple other religious traditions—with their own distinct cosmological orientations—ignored and disregarded by the dominant paradigm.[25] "Asian American religion refuses to be subsumed under the dominant methods and approaches of either Religious or Asian American studies as they have developed. This is why it is essential to acknowledge the constellation of relationships among colonialism, the plantation political economy, and the religious experiences," says Rudy Busto.[26]

Amphibolous faith is truly "hybrid," in the sense that hybridization is understood not as "'free' oscillation between or among chosen identities," but as "the uneven process through which immigrant communities encounter the violences of the U.S. state, . . . the process through which they survive those violences by living, inventing, and reproducing different cultural alternatives."[27] Amphibolous faith is "subaltern," unrealized and unrecognized by a wider community. Its history is fragmented, episodic, and identifiable only from a point of historical hindsight. The crucial thing is that those whose faith is amphibolous desire to be freed from oppressive ideologies and faith traditions that attempt to force them into an unwelcomed spiritual state. What is "revealed" in amphibology is the spiritual dynamics of Asian Americans, that is to

---

25. Busto describes Asian American spiritual beings as "disorienting self." See Busto, "Disorienting Subjects," 9–28.

26. Ibid., 24.

27. Lowe, *Immigrant Acts*, 82.

say, the paradox of America's claims to universality and the particularities silenced by those claims. People of amphibolous faith are driven by the desire for their broken history to not have the final say; they yearn for rehabilitative meaning and the restoration of the basic relatedness of people in a broken world. This desire for rapprochement is partially fulfilled through an excavation of their broken memories and histories, a necessary precondition for bringing those memories and histories into a liberative, healthy relationship. Amphibolous faith suggests that the alternative to blind belief is not simply unbelief but a different kind of belief, one that embraces uncertainty and enables us to respect others whom we do not understand. In a complex world, wisdom is knowing what we don't know so that we can keep the future open.

Out of an amphibolous faith emerges a yearning for reunion with unexcavated histories, unappreciated cultural norms, and disrupted relationships through a life of departure, distance, and return. It is a yearning that does not have a guarantee of being realized. Nevertheless, it is a strong yearning that does not goes away. Houston Smith's description of religion fittingly describes this strong yearning that dwells in an amphibolous faith: "Religions are like rivers, dynamic and changing, bearing the heritage of the past to water the fields of the present. These rivers are converging and we need to build bridges."[28] When Smith was once asked what we are to do with religion, he responded by saying, "We listen. We listen as alertly to the other person's description of reality as we hope they listen to us."[29] Amphibolous faith longs for the bridge-building through conversation whose real meaning is, as what Thomas Moore describes as puts it, "the interpretation of the worlds."

The primary challenge to democracy in the U.S. is a peoplehood that is devoid of the capacity to imagine life as others live it. In his presidential inauguration, Franklin Roosevelt talked about what democratic freedom is all about: "In this nation I see . . . millions of families trying to live on incomes so meager that the pall of family disaster hangs over them day by day. . . . The test of our progress is not whether we add more to the abundance of those who have much; it is whether we provide enough for those who have too little."[30] Roosevelt's bold assertion is echoed by George Semaan: the primary challenge facing

28. Smith, quoted in *Moyers on America*, 74.
29. Ibid., 74.
30. President Franklin Roosevelt's second inaugural address, (January 20, 1937).

America's peoplehood, based as it is on democratic freedom, is taking "into consideration the interests of others," particularly of those "who are weak and who have rights but are incapable of imposing these interests or these rights."[31] With characteristic insight, W. E. B. Du Bois articulated the "double consciousness" of African Americans as an alternate angle of vision for building the architecture of human relatedness, the peoplehood of America.[32] For Asian Americans, an alternate architecture of peoplehood derives from a second language forged out of the threefold epistemological scaffold of the racial construction that produces translocal morality, the dissonant' sensitivity to pathos in life, and amphibolous spirituality.

The Asian American "second language" is a hybrid, unfaithful to the dominant language of America.[33] It is also a language of deep empathy and compassion learned from the matrix of the "contradicting" experiences of being an American of Asian descent in a nation that prides itself on epitomizing democratic values but which does so through an array of homogenizing, universalizing practices. Thus, a second language has emerged from the very woundedness of Asian Americans' experiences, historically and even presently. In order to create a sustainable peoplehood at home and in our relations with world neighbors, serious attention must be paid to an interconnected web of people. But building a web of humanity is impossible without an honest acknowledgement of the real woundedness of America's highly racialized history, including the harmful racialization of our political and economic life. The serious challenges facing democratic governance are "questions of how and why some interests are allowed to dominate the government's decision making while others are excluded."[34] America faces "the never-ending work of democracy": the perplexing, sometimes bewildering, seemingly endless task of working through what kind of people we are going to be and what kind of communities we will live in and bequeath to our children and grandchildren. "We are creeping toward an oligarchic society where a relative handful of the rich and privileged decide, with their money, who will run, who will win, and how they will govern."[35] But

---

31. Semaan, quoted in James M. Wall, "Eyes to See," 45.
32. Du Bois, *Soul of the Black Folk*.
33. A representative articulation of a "second tongue" is Cha's *Dictee*.
34. Greider, *Who Will Tell the People*.
35. Smith, quoted in Moyers, *Moyers on America*, 102.

within America there are Asian American and other disfranchised communities that have created a second language out of their distinct angles of vision toward life in order to grasp the meaning of democracy. Such a second language begins with the acknowledgement of the harm that has been created in the name of democracy. The excavation of the historical injuries that have led to the emergence of such a second language will provide American peoplehood an important clue for its future.

The Original Language of American Peoplehood and Its Corruption

AN UNDERSTANDING OF THE rise of the Asian American second language begins with an analysis of our particular life orientation based on the threefold epistemological scaffold of translocal and rupturally liminal race identity, the spirit of dissonance and dissent, and amphibolous faith. For the understanding of the three pillars, we shall begin, first of all, with an examination of the "first language" spoken in the process of the establishment of this nation, the language behind the American democratic freedom. Following the publication of *Habits of the Heart,* sociologist Robert Bellah reflected on the theme of the book as he spoke about "A Common American Culture." While maintaining his original position of the dominant element of America's common culture, utilitarian individualism, as moderated by what he calls expressive individualism, Bellah later revised his original view: In the very core of utilitarian and expressive individualism lies "something very deep, very genuine, very old, very American, something we did not quite see or say in *Habits* . . . . That core is religious."[1] What Bellah means by this statement is that Roger Williams, and neither the Puritans nor John Winthrop as interpreted by Alexis de Tocqueville, really characterizes the common religious culture of America. "We are the only North Atlantic society whose predominant religious tradition is sectarian rather than an es-

---

1. Bellah, "Is There a Common American Culture?" 617.

tablished church."[2] And this idea of sectarianism originated in Roger Williams. Williams maintained "the absolute centrality of religious freedom, of the sacredness of individual conscience in matters of religious belief."[3] The vicissitudes of the sacredness of individual conscience eventually became embodies in the First Amendment of the Constitution and "has been given wider meaning by the judicial system, especially the Supreme Court, ever since."[4] Bellah points out that "something deeper in the American common culture of utilitarian or expressive individualism lies the sacredness of the individual conscience, of the individual person," embedded in the religious heritage of the Baptist tradition.

Roger Williams from whom this "American common culture" originated was indeed "a moral genius but he was a sociological catastrophe," says Bellah.[5] Why? Just when we are moving to an ever greater validation of the sacredness of the individual person, especially in the form of multiculturalism today, "our capacity to imagine a social fabric that would hold individual person is vanishing."[6] He says that the first language of America, democratic freedom, needs to be complemented by another language, that the language of the equality of all people. The "second languages" or second tongues of equality are spoken in certain quarters of the American society throughout our history. Bellah says that these languages that complements the first language of democracy have indeed held people together, "the languages of tradition and commitment in communities of memory . . . that most Americans know as well, and which they use when the language of the radically separate self does not seem adequate."[7] The second languages are expressed in such places as in the biblical and civic republican traditions. But Bellah questions whether Americans can reclaim second languages that complement our original language of the sacredness of individual conscience. The question is whether American democratic freedom can be sustainable in the world which is increasingly suspicious of what American democratic freedom has become lately in its mistreatment of our own people and in its strained relation to our world neighbors.

2. Ibid.
3. Ibid.
4. Ibid., Bellah quotes Hammond's book, *With Liberty for All*.
5. Ibid., 170.
6. Ibid.
7. Bellah, *Habits of the Heart*, 154.

Bellah say, "I was not very optimistic then (when he wrote *Habits of the Heart*); I am even less so today."[8]

H. Richard Niebuhr in *The Responsible Self* comments on the impact of the biblical tradition in the formation of the democratic freedom. The impact is the "cause of Christ" that is "the establishment of friendship between the power by which all things are and this human race of ours."[9] Niebuhr's message of the shaping power of history and the historical context of human choices is further emphasized in his *Christ and Culture*.

> Though we choose in freedom, we are not independent, for we exercise our freedom in the midst of values and powers we have not chosen but by which we are bound. Before we choose to live we have been chosen into existence, . . . have been elected members of humanity . . . . We have not chosen the time and place of our present, but we have been selected to stand at this post at this hour of watch or of battle. We have not chosen our culture . . . there has always been a choice prior to our own, and we live in dependence on it . . . The history of culture illustrates in myriad ways this dependence of our freedom on consequences we do not choose.[10]

In the writing Niebhur points out that in choosing freedom we pay a significant attention to our religious situation as well as to the value structures that condition our life in America. There are values, beliefs, or dispositions which are woven into the very fabric of our life and thought that shape whatever choices we make. There are values or dispositions of mind and modes of response which we hold simply because it has been our common force to come into existence in a particular geocultural and historical context in America. In the book *The Kingdom of God in America* Niebuhr again discusses the motifs of religious revolution that have had a great impact on American culture. He interpreted Christianity as a dynamic process in history rather than as simply a set of institutions. He noted a dialectical interplay between the relativism of human cultures and the basic beliefs of the Christian faith. But, caught up in the optimism of the age, the nation's founders heralded America as the land of promise and "no greater bliss" seemed available "than was

---

8. Bellah, "Is There A Common American Culture?" 622.
9. Niebuhr, *The Responsible Self,* 44–45.
10 Niebuhr, *Christ and Culture*, 249–51.

The Original Language of American Peoplehood and Its Corruption

afforded by the extension of American institutions to all the world."[11] With some derision, Niebuhr concluded that this positivistic vision of America "involved no discontinuities, no crises, no tragedies or sacrifices, no loss of all things, no cross and resurrection."[12] Niebuhr's claim in the book is that political and economic freedom cannot exist without a moral foundation, and the understanding of this moral foundation comes only from knowledge of God given in the religious context of the U.S. history. Moreover, a moral foundation needs to take into account the injuries that are embedded deep within our communal history and in our collective community of memory. This moral foundation is the equality of all people that is built not as a national ideal but on the tragic reminder of historical injuries that have been suffered by our own people in our knowledge of God. Niebuhr reminds us that the moral foundation based on this tragic "knowledge of God" is indeed America's representative second language, spoken to unite Americans into a peoplehood amidst the original language of the sacredness of individual conscience as truncated into utilitarian and expressive individualism.

But the rise of the original first language of this nation, democratic freedom, has undergone a gradual but a radical shift into the language of entitlement as expressed in terms of utilitarian and expressive individualism. The original language of the "Kingdom of God in America" with the memory of tragedy has become truncated. Furthermore, this original language resulted in a later development of the "Manifest Destiny" (the heaven smiles upon the new nation), or the idea of "A Go-Ahead Nation." The language was shaped in this Revolutionary tradition but was also based on a mutated set of values tempered by the Second Great Awakening.[13] The Civil War further strengthened this new set of values, the revolution of the first language, by relegating the Southerners to the status of "gentiles" in God's New Israel.[14] According to H. Richard Niebuhr, "America's destiny in the context of world history" is secularized and has become a progressive version of the original religious vision based on Edwards' millennialist notion of the Kingdom of God in America, the conception that has changed into a vision that "involved

11. Niebuhr, *The Kingdom of God in America*, 193.

12. Ibid.

13. "A God-Ahead Nation" was the term used by Johanssen of University of Notre Dame in his address at University of Illinois at Urbana-Champaign, 1998.

14. Bercovitch, *The Puritan Origins of the American Self*, 139.

no discontinuities, no crises, no tragedies or sacrifices, no loss of all things, no cross and resurrection."[15] This truncated version of the original religious vision is further morphed into a totalizing foundation of the nation and has been furthermore, racialized, politicized, and became a "colonializer" in the American context. What has emerged out of this process of the shift in the fundamental values is the language of utilitarian individualism coupled with expressive individualism without any discernable memories of tragedy that tell painful stories of shared suffering that creates deeper identities than success and competitiveness. This shift has been oppressive to many while seemingly beneficial to a privileged few. The totalized history of this truncated Christian faith is often too narrowly confined, brittle, and does not speak to those whose existence have been dismissed or ignored and are just recently beginning to claim their own agency and representation in today's world. It is especially problematic on two interrelated accounts: its particularized re-definition of Christian faith canonized and universalized in the form of atomic individualism, and, secondly, its neglect, if not an abuse, of the second language of human equality. This triumphalistic redefinition of the particular Christian religious and philosophical paradigm has been construed as normative and definitive in speaking of Christian faith that has resulted in what Canadian theologian Douglas John Hall calls America as "an officially optimistic society."[16]

Today, the preservation of democratic freedom coupled with the incorporation of the original second language and other languages is increasingly becoming difficult. There are some telltale signs of the credibility chasm that separates Americans from the confidence self-assurance that once pervaded our national experience of our "officially optimistic" nation. Historian Martin Marty noted a shift began in mid-1950s with an emerging consciousness of pluralism that was further reinforced by the immigration reform of 1966.[17] Furthermore, a gradual erosion of the public confidence in our foreign and military policies in recent decades after World War II, an ambivalence regarding our globalized economic system that seems to widen the gap between the poor and the rich, and eroding the confidence in financial institutions, suspicions over religion, race, ethnicity, gender, and sexuality differences provide

15. Niebuhr, *The Kingdom of God in America*, 191.
16. Hall, *Lighten the Darkness*.
17. Marty, *Religion and Republic*.

The Original Language of American Peoplehood and Its Corruption

visual evidence of disequilibrium. Bellah cautions that a recovery of such a "sacred convention" does not necessarily work in today's America because the context from which the sacred convention arose, namely the sectarian persecuted groups, is not appreciated and valued in the dominant American culture.[18] Sydney Ahlmstrom's warning almost three decades ago rings true more so today than ever before: "... a large portion of the American population ... are virtually excluded from the implicit social contract which provides the basis of their loyalty."[19] He went on to say:

> In the complicated root system that nourishes American social evils, two roots are of manifestly special significance. One of them is endemic in the human race—and we call it racism. It destroys our sense of community by keeping human beings and human groups irrationally and obsessively at odds with one another, and always to the greatest detriment of the weaker person and groups. The other is endemic in the United States of America as in no other land ..., and it may be called rampant anarchic economic individualism [RAE], which destroys our sense by community by keeping human beings in a perpetual state of competition and instability from kindergarten to cemetery, and which also by the creation of corporate "persons" keeps cities, states, suburbs, regions, and neighborhoods in destructive contexts of unnecessarily rapid social change, which in turns conduces to immeasurable amounts of human woes and to the general institutional instability and insolvency.[20]

Both these words of H. Richard Niebhur's and Sydney Ahlstrom are prophetic in their cautions against the erosion of the moral foundations of the society today. "A God without wrath brought men [sic] without sin into a kingdom without judgment through the ministrations of a Christ without a cross," says Niebuhr.[21] A social contract that is the basis of a sacred convention for the society is possible only when the disfranchised segments of the society are included in it in the name of equality, in other words, when the peoplehood is built on their languages, America's second languages, that are appreciated and valued. To accomplish such an inclusion will involve both an acknowledgement of human finitude

---

18. Bellah, "Is There a Common American Culture?" 618.
19. Ahlstrom, *Religious History*, 22.
20. Ibid., 21.
21. Niebhur, *The Kingdom of God in America*.

and sensitivity toward suffering, and "tragedy," which become eroded when the moral foundation of the society becomes self-serving by its separation from the original context.

An assault on the original language of democratic freedom based on the new language of self-entitlement is further intensified in our current climate of fear. Cornel West in his *Democracy Matters: Winning the Fight Against Imperialism* warns the "prevailing dogmas" that lead to a deeply troubling deterioration of democratic powers in America today, free-market fundamentalism, aggressive militarism, and escalating authoritarianism. Together these dogmas are

> snuffing out the democratic impulses that are so vital for the deepening and spread of democracy in the world. In short, we are experiencing the sad American imperial devouring of American democracy. This historic devouring in our time constitutes an unprecedented gangsterization of America—an unbridled grasp at power, wealth, and status. And when the most powerful forces in a society—and an empire—promote a suffocation of democratic energies, the very future of genuine democracy is jeopardized.[22]

West calls for serious and thorough ideological and material reconstructions to fight against these dogmas. Such a task should begin, in part, with the critical reassessment of the American religious tradition. Without that reevaluation, Americans will suffer a deepening sense of fatalism, and drift, willy-nilly, toward an ever greater loss of social morale and coherence.

George Semaan's challenge, to "change its perspective on how it builds its interests and how it defends them, by building a network of relationships that takes into consideration the interests of others who are weak and who have rights but are incapable of imposing these interests or these rights," speaks to this crisis of democracy in the U.S. It is not only directed toward the foreign policies of the current U.S. administration. It questions the "sacred conventions" of this society, namely the deeply held and shared national values of "life, liberty, and the pursuit of happiness" in light of the increasing social disequilibrium that is taking place both at home and abroad. Without complementing the societal valuation of the equality of all people as spoken in America's second languages to the first language of democracy, we need to ask ourselves: Are our national principles of "life, liberty, and the pursuit of happiness"

---

22. West, *Democracy Matters*, 8.

that have become more of an entitlement, sustainable in an increasingly interconnected, and at the same time, woefully fragmented world of ours where people are alienated one from another? If indeed the civic virtue of equality of all people is to be recovered, what adjustments and modifications need to be made in order to cope with a genuine dislike of the power America wields around the world?

In order to respond to these questions, Americans need to recognize and appreciate signs in our midst, though still faint, of suggesting societal conventions that could be considered for the future of the U.S. in the increasingly interrelated and simultaneously fractured world of ours. Such emerging social conventions in the form of second languages are democratic but not coercive. They are religious in nature but not in an exclusive fashion based on a particular historical religious tradition such as Puritanism and the Edwardsian millennialism. New languages that are gradually emerging in America are not the language of the "Kingdom of God." Rather, new languages of peoplehood in America are deeply religious without explicitly being associated with a particular historical religion. They are likely to be fragile but, at the same time, durable. Such a language is likely to be found in numerous but previously unnoticed places. These languages are likely rooted in an often ignored and dismissed lived experiences of those who are outside of the dominant communities, particularly among economically, culturally, religiously, and racially undervalued and disfranchised people. But the revaluation of the second languages of America, the alternate civic and religious values that lead to the recovery of American peoplehood, may slowly accomplish a revolution as profound as Puritanism's erosion of the grounds for popular acceptance of the old authoritarian structures of English government. John Adams once observed that "The Revolution was in the minds and hearts of the people; a change in their religious sentiments of their duties and obligations."[23] Jose Ortega y Gasset noted that order is not pressure that is imposed on a society from without, but an equilibrium that is set up from within. A revolution may indeed be taken place quietly in the minds and hearts of some Americans today, particularly those whose worldviews and life-perspectives have been undervalued. And yet, significant and real changes in the cohering values of the American society are gradually shaped in the experiences of

---

23. Koch and Peden, eds., *The Selected Writings of John and John Quincy Adams*, 203–5.

those who are living by such alternate sets of values, a different language, from the one we are used to speak as a nation, as a people. The recent speech by Barack Obama, then a presidential candidate, on race is one powerful example of the emergence of a set of alternate civic and religious values.[24] His speech called Americans to rediscover the civic values articulated in the Declaration of Independence, "We the people, in order to form a more perfect union," in today's highly pluralistic society. Being cast on the subject of race as a "stalemate" in America, Obama called for this nation to address the racial divide in a way that "continue the long march of those who came before us, a march for a more just, more equal, more free, more caring and more prosperous America." Obama in his campaign speech calls for "the realization, the comprehension and fulfillment of what was taken to be America's destiny in the context of world history," says historian Bernard Bailyn.[25] Obama challenges American to move away from the truncated notion of democratic freedom as an entitlement to the recovery of the original vision of America, "that we do unto others as we would have them do unto us. Let us be our brother's keeper, Scripture tells us. Let us be our sister's keeper. Let us find that common state we all have in one another, and let our politics reflect that spirit as well."[26] He calls for American to recover the original second languages that have been long lost with the aid of a new set of second languages, the languages spoken in disfranchised and undervalued groups of Americans. But the understanding of these new second languages requires the painful realization of "tragedy" that we are all complicit in the use of our first language, American radical individualism. The story of American peoplehood is an unfolding one. America was founded and "dedicated," according to Abraham Lincoln in his Gettysburg Address "to equality as a "self-evident truth." But this very principle of equality was a "proposition" as Abraham Lincoln noted. To make it reality remained the unfinished work of Americans.

---

24. Obama's speech given on March 18, 2008 in Philadelphia, PA.
25. Quoted in Kennerman, "America's Best Leaders 2009," 11.
26. Ibid.

2

People On the Way

Translocal and Rupturally Liminal Experience of Race

THE LANGUAGE SPOKEN IN Asian American communities is indeed a second language of America. The understanding of the Asian American language begins with an exploration of our experiences of race. Historical Ronald Takaki uses the term "a different mirror" to describe America's second languages that racially and culturally minoritized people of America use for their experiences of race.[1] The epic story of America seen and told in a different mirror is not the epic story told from the top-down, the perspectives of the rich and powerful. It is the story told from the bottom-up, through the lives, experiences, and stories of everyday people. Their varied voices, orchestrated side-by-side together, tell the complicated but hopeful story of America as peopled by the world.

Asian Americans' experiences of race are the story told in a different mirror. Race is a powerful site for Asian Americans' reading of memory, identity, and value orientation. It is a major source of our second language based on our "community of memory." For Asian Americans race is translocal in character and nomadic or "rupturally liminal" in value orientation. Race is also the locus of a vision of life that "involved . . . discontinuities, . . . crises, . . . tragedies or sacrifices, . . . loss of all things, . . . cross and resurrection," to paraphrase H. Richard Niebuhr's reading of the "moral foundation" of a democratic society. In

---

1. Takaki, *A Different Mirror*.

this chapter, the translocal character of race and the nomadic or "rupturally liminal" value orientation of Asian American's experience of race are explored. Together the translocal and nomadic notions of race speak to the emergence of Asian Americans' second language.

RACE AS BEING TRANSLOCAL

The translocality of race is reflected in the designation Asian Americans give to ourselves, the "People on the Way." Asian Americans are indeed a "People on the Way," living amidst a myriad of racialized experiences of contradictions, injured bodies and souls, fluidity about our identities, and the experiences that deepen one's sense of human frailty, and yet we stubbornly refuse to be overcome by the frailty and futility of life.[2] Asian Americans continue to walk the destabilized, transitory, and translocal path of life, the "Way." It is much more than the sum of what our experiences, individually and communally, may teach us. The Way reveals to us the meaning of life far deeper than our own insights can grant us, far larger than we can comprehend. The Way leads us to say "Even though I couldn't find a solution now, it didn't mean there wasn't one. I must be patient and learn to resign myself to waiting. There is a time for effort and a time for repose; a time for knowledge and a time for ignorance. At present time all I could do was wait with an alert mind."[3] We are indeed "People on the Way" both in our racialized experiences of historical injuries and in our lived-life postures that refuse to be defeated by the injuries. Asian Americans wait with "an alert mind" as we go on the Way is our race experiences. In the process, our own racialized stories of identity and racial formations de-legitimize the conventional notion of multiculturalism that reduces the cultural differences to a level plain field, the ideology of equivalency of differences that negates the power-differentials that exists among racialized groups of people. Asian Americans as "People on the Way" tell our own story of our identities, suggesting "translocality" that is never fully measurable by the same standard among the differences. Translocality that characterizes the "People on the Way" is a reading of our racialized material life that is both contradictory and insurgent in character, contradictory to the

---

2. Omi and Winant, *Racial Formation*; and Ng, ed., *People on the Way*.
3. Ha Jin, *War Trash*.

prevailing dominant reading of history and is insurgent in exposing the limit of the conventional level-playing field reading of racial diversity.

Race indeed matters for us Asian Americans because race is linked to the emergence of Asian Americans' second language, the excavation of our collective and individual memories, identities, and our own representations in a racialized society. Our experiences of race have contradicted the publicly stated "truth" of equality in America. To be sure, Asian Americans remind ourselves that a claim for our own identity and representation is "a point of departure and not ultimately about arrival."[4] This is to say that race as we Asian Americans experience is really a means to provide a clue for our second language that speaks of peoplehood, in which we are part. To understand the function of race as a point of departure to discuss American peoplehood, a probe into the connection between race and the "self-evident truth" of equality is needed. For Asian Americans, the character of race as we experience is what Lisa Lowe calls "*continuing material contradictions*" in which Asian American collective identities and values are forged and claimed.[5] What does she mean by race that is "contradictory"? By this term Lowe means that race is "a contradictory site of struggle for cultural, economic, as well as political membership in the United States:

> . . . the history of the nation's attempt to resolve the contradictions between its economic and political imperatives through laws that excluded Asians from citizenship—from 1790 until the 1940s—contributes to our general understanding of *race* as a contradictory site of struggle for cultural, economic, as well as political membership in the United States.[6]

Rather than confirming a traditional anthropological model of "cultural identity" in which a particular culture or ethnicity is passed from generation to generation, Asian American identities are better understood as racialized ways in which our identities are imagined, practiced, and continued among communities and are transmitted in re-

---

4. Yoon quoted by Kim in "Room Viewed From a Marginal Site.
5. Lowe, *Immigrant Acts*.
6. Ibid., ix. Lowe defines "Immigrant acts," to mean "attempts to name the *contradictions* of Asian immigration, which at different moments in the last century and a half of Asian entry into the United States have placed Asians 'within' the U.S. nation-state, its workplaces, and its markets, yet linguistically, culturally, and racially marked Asians as 'foreign' and 'outside' the national polity" (8).

markably fragile and fragmented ways from one generation to the next. Race is that "contradictory site of struggle" for Asian Americans. The material contradictions of the national economy and the political state are expressed in the legal exclusion, disenfranchisement, and restricted enfranchisement of Asian immigrants. Our experiences of racialization are the "material site of struggle" in which active links are made between "signifying practices and social structure that supports the practices."[7] Race as such a "site" rests on both the history of how the United States, its foreign policies, immigration, and citizenship laws were created, and how these public policies and regulatory laws have shaped views of "being American," and the meaning of what constitutes "America." Race as a "material site of struggle" is "translocal" in Asian Americans' experiences. We have experienced race as translocality in terms representatively of (1) being labeled as "Orientals" and (2) living in an oscillation between two contradictory images of "a model minority" and "foreigners within."

Translocality of Being "Orientals"

The history of America and how America has come to understand what it means to be an American in international relations have affected how Asian Americans have come to be perceived by a wider public and, equally, how we Asian Americans understand our own identities. We begin with simple questions: What is the difference between being an "Oriental" and an "Asian American"? How have these terms come to be used? Why do some people prefer to use a more ethnically based term such as an "Korean American" or "Filipino American" rather than a more inclusive "Asian American'? At the time when out-marriage, a marriage across racial and ethnicity lines, is so rampant, can we realistically talk about an "Asian American" as a racialized and ethnic group?

In order to respond to these questions, we begin with the relationship between the construction of Asian American identities and U.S. immigration and foreign policies. Race experienced as "translocal" by Asian Americans begin in this connection. For researchers in many areas of ethnic studies, the ways race is constructed in the U.S. have long been an important focus. Michael Omi and Howard Winant talk about "racial formation" to approach the study of race in the United States. They define racial formation as "the sociohistorical process by which

---

7. Ibid., 22.

racial categories are created, inhabited, transformed, and destroyed."[8] In other words, race is "a matter of both social structure and cultural representation." "A racial project is simultaneously an interpretation, representation, or explanation of racial dynamics, and effort to reorganize and redistribute resources along particular racial lines."[9] Race for Omi and Winant is representation that is embedded in the social structure of the United States. This is a very useful approach to understand Asian Americans' experience of race. In recent years scholars in American studies are asking the question of how the American quest for empire has historically influenced definitions of race and ethnicity in the United States.[10] The language of international relations reveals, and is even based on, racial and gender prejudices, argues historian Emily S. Rosenberg.[11] The borderland studies of recent decades also link the study of ethnicity and immigration inextricably to the study of international relations and empire. Foreign relations do not take place outside the national boundaries but rather constitute American nationality. Christina Klein of Massachusetts Institute of Technology points out, for example, that Hawaii presents a fascinating kind of borderland, an Asian Pacific borderland. During the Cold War, the U.S. "had to define itself as a global power in a big way. As part of that, it had to define itself as a racially inclusive nation back home."[12] So, in the 1950s, Hawaii was cast as a paradise of racial tolerance. U.S. officials hoped that image would reassure Asian nations dubious about American expansionism. They talked of Hawaii as a bridge into Asia, and described its statehood as a sign of mainland American's acceptance of Hawaii's large Asian population. James Michener's novel, *Hawaii* (1959) was published in the same year that statehood was granted. The novel showed a Hawaii becoming more tolerant, and told classic, and ethnic-immigrant stories of overcoming hardships. The reality was not so rosy, however. The racial and ethnic make-ups of the Hawaiian population are much more complex. The economically and politically based power hierarchy of Hawaii was closely tied with the intricate ethnically and racially defined groups competing

---

8. Omi and Winant, *Racial Formation*, 55.
9. Ibid., 56.
10. One such work is Kramer, *The Blood of Government*.
11. Rosenberg, *Spreading the American Dream*.
12. Kleine, *Cold War Orientalism*, 270.

with each other. But the romanticized image of Hawaii served as a powerful instrument of U.S. foreign policy in the backdrop of the Cold War.

But the root of the intersection between U.S. foreign policies, immigration, and citizenship laws on one hand and the construction of race and gender in America on the other goes beyond the recent history. This country was founded on the clashing and mixing of many different races, cultures, and lifestyles, often in a very painful way. The annihilation of Native Americans, the enslavement of Africans, and the brutal treatment of Hispanic, Asian and Pacific Islander Americans are embedded in our national psyche. On the international scene, after the Philippines-American War of 1898, Americans came to describe Filipinos as "like the Indians" and as "savages." After all, 80% of U.S. troops sent into the conflict were veterans of the American Indian wars. They simply borrowed from existing stereotypes of American Indians to cast Filipinos as "others."[13] Paul Kramer's description of how the Filipino representatives were treated at the 1904 World's Fair in St. Louis, Missouri, is instructive.[14] At the fair, the Filipino Village was a symbol of American empire. Dressed in U.S. military uniforms, Filipino constables tromped up and down to the triumphalistic din of John Philip Sousa. The display was intended to make the case, to both liberal critics and racist imperialists, that the U.S. colonization of the Philippines had been a "good idea." The occupying governors' message to their fellow Americans was: "These people aren't so savage that we can't do anything with them." They wanted the constabulary to put on a show of civilization—an orderly one. But the first thing the scouts did, when they got out onto the fairgrounds was to flirt with white women and outraged white segregationalists of the day, reports Kramer.[15]

The U.S. colonial government set up bureaus of anthropologists whom the government pushed to serve as intermediaries with native tribes. But they were criticized by Filipino elites—people who had studied in Paris and other similar centers of the West. When it came time to select the Filipino ambassadors to the 1904 World's Fair, the elite Filipinos complained about the selections, saying, "you're taking the most savage people to display." They pressed the government to bring representatives of the elites to St. Louis. But that plan backfired.

13. Sobredo et al., *Studies in Pacific History*.
14. Kramer, *The Blood of Government*.
15. Ibid.

American public wasn't interested in talking to the elites: they gravitated to the native villages. The elites soon came to believe that Americans' appetite for the exotic might not be such a bad thing. It would, they concluded, win better U.S. treatment of the Philippines than the elites' own sophistication in Western ways.[16]

The events at the Filipino Village reveal some of the many tensions of empire. The question is not just how the U.S. has influenced the world, but also how its experience occupying other nations shaped ideas about the meaning of "America" and "Americans." How have Americans construed such concepts as race and rights in such countries as the Philippines and former colonial possessions such as Hawaii? How are American notions of citizenship related to the U.S. actions in countries it colonized, and whose peoples later sought to immigrate to the U.S.? The way race is constructed is an important focus for the studies of U.S. foreign policies. Lisa Lowe, for one, argues that U.S. Immigrant and citizenship laws and other expressions of culture and society have left Asian Americans forever suspended between foreignness—their status as "Asians"—and full citizenship in the U.S.[17] This dual position stems not only from racial prejudices but also from a warped view of Asia leading to the treatment of Asian Americans as a translocal people, whose identity is translocally suspended between the two poles, an "Asian" and an "American."

Asia has been always a complex site on which the manifold anxieties of the U.S. nation-state have been figured: such anxieties have figured Asian countries as exotic, barbaric, and alien, and Asian laborers immigrating to the U.S. from the 19th century onward as a "Yellow Peril" threatening to displace white European immigrants.[18] Even as Asian immigrants have been taken into workplaces, markets, and other areas of U.S. society, Asian American have remained "foreigners-within." Therefore, for Lisa Lowe, Asian America is a cultural site "where the contradictions of immigrant history are read, performed, and criticized."[19] Elaine H. Kim of the University of California at Berkeley also sees this connection between the U.S. foreign policy abroad and the treatment of Asian Americans at home. Kim notes that there is a commonality

16. Ibid.
17. Lowe, *Immigrant Acts*.
18. Ibid.
19. Ibid., 5.

between American images of Korean women as sex workers around U.S. bases in the Korean War and their poor treatment in factories and offices in the U.S. today. Both reflect the physicality of Korean women in the context of exploited labor.[20] Kim explores a problematic gender construction that originates in Korea, and extends even today to Korean communities beyond Asia. Stereotyped representations of Korean women still attempt to confine them to the status of either mother or prostitute.

The "racialization of savagery" abroad and demonizing of racial and ethnic groups at home are deeply rooted in the history of the U.S. and are juxtaposed with the contrary and optimistic national motto expressed in the Bill of Rights for every person. The notion of "life, liberty and the pursuit of happiness for all" is for racially underprivileged groups of people a painful reminder of their unequalized social status coupled with the historical disparity of power and potentials that exist between these groups and the racially powerful dominant Anglo European Americans. This discrepancy between the stated national slogan and the material contradiction of the society has created not only the sense of resentment but, more importantly, an oppositional, not a complementary, dynamic in relationships among Americans across racial lines thus creating the current deep racial divides. It seems that the increasingly adversarial ways in Americans relate with each other today across the racial, ethnic, religious lines is a reflection of this historical reality of disparity and alienation. The primary force of the conflict and distrust across racial, class, religious and ideological lines is reflected in the ideal of Manifest Destiny and the ways in which land was to be tamed and conquered by those who are powerful both at home and abroad. The treatment of the people of color has been harsh, cruel, and violent to say the least in such places as Philippines and American Indian reservations just as in the history of African Americans. It is in this treatment of the people of color that Americans has come to view the racially undervalued people as a "racialized other" and where race began to matter and an oppositional dynamic of relationship began to surface in the American peoplehood and in its international relationships. This early thinking as it is symbolized in the Manifest Destiny is what created our American identity based on race. In the early settling of this country, when the English first encountered the Indians they viewed them as uncivilized

20. Kim and Choi, eds., *Dangerous Women*.

beasts. "The first English colonizers in the New World found that the Indians reminded them of the Irish."[21] To the English the Irish represented a lower and uncivilized class of people, a group that the English considered to be beneath them. For Asian Americans, race is equally a historical signifier of this oppositional dynamic, a racialized other. This meaning of race is expressed as translocal enigma in the contradictions between the economic and political imperatives of the government through laws that excluded Asians from citizenship and also the reality of the actual presence of Asian American citizens in this society. It is the contradiction that has contributed to Asian Americans' experience of race as being translocal, a contradictory site of struggle for cultural, economic, as well as political membership in the United States.

Being "Orientals Within"

However, there is a further complexity in describing the translocal character of race for Asian Americans. It is a peculiar internal dynamic operating within Asian American communities that also perpetuates the experience of race as being translocal. The issue is how Asian Americans have internalized within ourselves the binary Orientalized perception imposed from outside. The term "Orientalism" as coined by Edward Said is that knowledge about the East is generated not through actual facts, but through imagined constructs that see "Eastern" societies as being all fundamentally similar, all sharing crucial characteristics that are not possessed by "Western" societies.[22] Thus, this *a priori* knowledge sets up the East as the antithesis of the West. Such knowledge is constructed through literary texts and historical records that are often limited in terms of their understanding of the actualities of life in the Middle East or Asia. A mythical Orient was used to justify and implement European and American colonialism.[23] The epistemological assumption of Orientalism is thus a binary reading of human relationship that is being cast in terms of a wider political and cultural power differential.

> My contention is that Orientalism is fundamentally a political doctrine willed over the Orient because the Orient was weaker than the West, which elided the Orient's difference with its weak-

---

21. Jeung, *Faithful Generations*, 28.
22. Said, *Orientalism*.
23. Ibid.

ness . . . As a cultural apparatus Orientalism is all aggression, activity, judgment, will-to-truth, and knowledge."[24]

The "Orientalized" Asian Americans, regardless of their national and ethnic origins, thus have come to be lumped together as "Orientals" in politically and racially binary fashion.[25] This history of American Orientalism that has helped to produce modern notions of race and culture also arose from studying "Orientals," connected by social scientists with theories about Asian Americans and white European immigrants. Simultaneously, this Orientalized perception of Asian Americans also has impacted the internal psyche of Asian Americans ourselves.

Henry Yu's work builds on *Orientalism*, Edward Said's study, to describe how the internalized Orientalism operates within Asian American communities. Yu uses poignant vignettes to illustrate the difficult and often ironic positions of intellectuals of color. One of these vignettes speak of an Chinese American intellectual providing a glimpse into an Asian American version of W. E. B. Du Bois's notion of the "veil" and "double consciousness" of racialized people in the U.S. The story is that of the life of a Chinese American sociologist Rose Hum Lee. Lee engaged in research on the subject of "Orientals in America" and the role of cultural translator and the marginal existence of Chinese Americans. Lee saw the assimilation of Chinese Americans into the mainstream U.S. society and the corresponding eradication of physical and cultural distinction as the only way to eliminate both the racial prejudice of the European Americans and the clannish tendencies of many Chinese Americans. In this sense, Lee was a product of the Chicago School on the matter of race. "Rose Hum Lee's sociological outlook and career gave her a valuable intellectual and emotional distance from the Oriental community that she wanted so desperately to leave behind."[26] However, Lee was unexpectedly ostracized by the Chinese American community of Chicago, her own community, not so much for her own sociological stance as her distance from it by her educational attainment.

"I shall never forget the faces of the women in Chinatown when they heard me say I got my Ph.D. The look of envy and greed came forth and instead of congratulating me for having arrived after years of strug-

---

24. Ibid., 204.
25. Yu, *Thinking Orientals*.
26. Ibid., 132.

gle and sacrifice and malicious gossiping about my 'loose ways,' they smirked. I guess, too, they're mad because I don't socialize with them. Well, I'll never do that now."[27] Lee's experience demonstrates a double bind that Asian Americans find ourselves in, the perception of being "Oriental" from the white society and the distance and alienation from her own communities by being associated closely with and assimilated into the racially dominant group. This is another expression of race being translocal for Asian Americans. By analyzing two movements, first, how some European American intellectuals wanting to know about "Orientals" which helped define themselves as white, and secondly, how Asian Americans deal with this perception, think about it, survive, and at times even thrive within a structure built upon the curiosity of European Americans, the double bind, translocality, in which Asian Americans are placed is revealed. This double bind is what Said labels the "second order of Orientalism." Asian Americans shape the possibilities of meaning by using the power of Orientalist knowledge itself. In other words, Asian Americans "Orientalize" ourselves (second order). This is in contrast to the long history of how people in Europe and the United States created the idea of an "Orient" that was the opposite of everything "Occidental" (first order). A theoretical metaphor for identity, "calling skin color a costume or a mask," emphasized race as a set of acts performed in front of non-Asian audiences. The social possibilities that such a dramatic language allowed for Asian Americans were limited by the demand for Oriental performances, so that non-Asian Americans established the market for what was valuable. There was room for Asian American intellectuals to maneuver, to negotiate, and to choose different paths for understanding. However such a maneuver is a highly constrained set of roles. The reality of these constraints and what non Asian Americans say about the ways that American intellectuals treated race and culture in the last century is precisely the legacy of "Asian American Orientalism." Cultural theory became confused with anti-racism, and a color-blind denial of race has failed to free us from racism, making the identity affirmation of Asian Americans highly problematic. Furthermore, this "Orientals Within" is expressed among Asian Americans as *nativism*, the split between American-born Asians and immigrants with the sense of superiority implied on the side of those who are American-born.

27. Ibid., 133 (quoted from Rose Hum Lee's private correspondence, dated January 8, 1958, in the possession of Elaine Lee and the author).

Therefore, race defined by Lowe for Asian Americans as "a contradictory site of struggle for cultural, economic, as well as political membership in the United States" is a useful way of understanding its complexity. Race for Asian Americans is indeed translocal in so many dimensions of life.

Translocality Between "Model Minority" and "Foreigners Within/Yellow Perils"

Just as the relationship between the history of U.S. foreign policies, immigration, and citizenship laws shapes the construction of the translocal Asian American's identity and frames Asian Americans' "cultural site," an equally significant force contributing to our identity formation is the interaction among various racially disfranchised groups of Americans on the domestic front. Historian Gary Okihiro poses a question, "Is Yellow Black or White?"[28] This question reflects not only an ambiguous and translocal role Asian Americans hold in this racialized society but also pertains to the question of American peoplehood as a whole and the disturbing nature of America's racial formation.

It is by now a well-known observation that by seeing only a black and white binary in race relations while ignoring all other races, white renders Asians, American Indians, African Americans and Latinos invisible ignoring the gradations and complexities of the full spectrum between the racial poles. At the same time, it is equally true that Asian Americans share with African Americans the status and repression of nonwhites as the racially "Other." Therein lies what Okihiro terms the "debilitating aspect of Asian-African antipathy" and a possibly liberating nature of African-Asian Unity.[29] To be sure, the irreducibility of race applies distinctly and appropriately to African American experiences of race and racism. This is so because their distinct history of forced slavery, and their involuntary introduction to the U.S., renders to the special significance of race for them unlike other racialized groups of Americans. To ignore this reality is to relative the U.S. racial scene and to do injustice to the distinctness of African Americans' racialization. Equally, it is necessary to note that the ambivalence associated with the positioning of Asian Americans in the U.S. landscape of race--the "foreigners within" and a "model minority" images--has its own dis-

---

28. Okihiro, "Is Yellow Black or White?" 63–78.
29. Ibid., 75.

tinctness. The ambivalence originates from how we have been treated in the history of racial formation in the U.S. There are periods in the history of the U.S. when both African and Asian work forces were seen related insofar as they were both essential for the maintenance of white supremacy. "[T]hey were both members of an oppressed class of 'colored' laborers, and they were both tied historically to the global network of labor migration as slaves and coolies."[30] An early Korean immigrant writer, Younghill Kang (1903–1972), in his novel, *East Goes West* has a revealing description of this identification of African Americans and Asian Americans. The novel is the chronicle of the main character, Han, and his continual search for the fictional America he had constructed within his own imagination: it is an idea, a "mental utopia," a place of regeneration, a dream full of magic and mastery, a "glorious vision" of enchantment and romance, a spiritual home.[31] The search is unsuccessful and ends with a nightmare:

> And now as is the inconsequential way of dreams, I was running down the steps into a dark and cryptlike cellar, still looking for my money and my keys. The cellar seemed to be under the pavements of a vast city. Other men were in that cellar with me, some frightened-looking Negroes, I remember. Then looking back, I saw, through an iron grating into the upper air, men with clubs and knives. The cellar was being attacked. The Negroes were about to be mobbed. I shut the door and bolted it, and called to my frightened fellows to help me hold the door. "Fire, bring fire," called the red-faced men outside. And through the grating I saw the flaring torches being brought. And applied. Being shoved, crackling, through the gratings. I awoke like a phoenix out of a burst of flames. I have remembered this dream because according to Oriental interpretation, it is a dream of good omen. To be killed in a dream means success, and in particular death by fire augurs good fortune. This is supposed to be so, because death symbolizes in Buddhistic philosophy growth and rebirth and a happier reincarnation.[32]

The disappointment, misunderstanding, loneliness, and alienation that Han experienced in this society are shared experiences between Asian and African Americans, "nonwhites." Some of the first inhabitants

---

30. Ibid., 68.
31. Kang, *East Goes West*.
32. Ibid., 400–401.

of South and Southeast Asia were a people called "Negrito." White planters in the nineteenth century saw Chinese laborers as the "coinheritors with the Negroes of the lowliness of caste, the abuse, the ruthless exploitation." "I look upon the introduction of Chinese on our Rice lands, & especially on the unhealthy cotton lands as new and essential machines in the room of others that have been destroyed [or are] wearing out, year by year."[33] Some African Americans recognized early on the wide embrace of racism and equated racism directed at Asians with racism directed at Africans. Frederick Douglass declared that the southern planters' scheme to displace African with Asian labor was stimulated by the same economic and racist motives that supported the edifice of African Slavery and they believe in it still.[34] The status of "nonwhites" that was given both to Africans and Asians was institutionalized in American policies and proposed legislations, may it be slavery or exclusionary immigration policies.

On the other hand, Asian Americans were sometimes paradoxically classified as whites in order to insulate whites from African Americans. In the post-Civil War South Asians were considered as replacements for African Americans precisely because they were not African Americans and were thus perpetual foreigners. The contemporary notion of the "model minority" perception of Asian Americans maintains its underlying assumption that Asian Americans are "near whites" or "whiter than whites," even though in this minority stereotype we continue to experience racism like African Americans and other racially disfranchised groups of people in occupational barriers. Such an ambiguous state of race classification of Asian Americans has resulted in a confused image of who we are in the racial hierarchy of the U.S. and, simultaneously, created opportunities for an alliance with other racially oppressed groups of people.

What Okihiro terms the "debilitating aspect of Asian-African antipathy" is further exacerbated by the U.S. government's efforts to treat Asians as racially diverse ethnic groupings rather than a single racialized category. While Asian immigrants were long excluded for naturalization into citizenship in the U.S., there were certain exceptions that were made to whites-only barrier. Such an exception, according to Legal scholar

---

33. Okihiro, *Margins and Mainstreams*, 44. Quoted from Roak, *Master without Slave*, 167.

34. Okihiro, *Margins and Mainstreams*, 48.

Neil Gotanda, resulted in fragmented ethnicity-based categorization of Asian immigrants thus supporting and obscuring at the same time the powerful centrality of the white racial category.[35] This is to say, "through the legal enfranchisement of specific Asian ethnic groups as *exceptions* to the whites-only classification, the status of Asians as *nonwhite* is legally restated and reestablished. Thus, the historical racialization of Asian-origin immigrants as nonwhite aliens ineligible to citizenship is actually rearticulated in the process of legal enfranchisement and the ostensive lifting of legal discrimination in the 1950s."[36] In more recent years, another complication in the racial formation of Asian Americans has emerged. It is the spectrum of color that exists within Asian American communities, from East Asians to South Asians, with its corresponding economic, social, and educational disparities. A new racial fault line created in the aftermath of the tragic events of September 11, 2001, classifies subgroups within Asian Americans according to the assumed hostility and danger these subgroups of people might pose to the national security. Following the immigration reform act of 1965 that reclassified Asians within a broad segment of racialized immigrants, the target of particularized classification by the U.S. Immigration Service shifted to "alien" and "undocumented" Mexican and Latino workers. By so doing, the official shift in the classification signaled a legitimization of racial classification of another disfranchised group in the eye of the society. Gotanda describes the racialization of Asian Americans in terms of a multiple model over against the comparative model of racialization that applies to the black/white relationship.[37] The Asian American narratives of their collective memories of exclusion now serve as a powerful instrument for a "larger memory" of liberal democracy in the U.S., this time, for the newly disfranchised people. Asians, like African Americans, resisted their exploitation and subjugation, and in the shared struggle for equality secured the blessings of democracy for all peoples. On this point, we must be clear. Inclusion, human dignity, and civil rights are not "black issues," nor are they gains for one group made at the expense of

---

35. Gotanda, "Towards Repeal of Asian Exclusion."

36. Lowe, *Immigrant Acts*, 20.

37. Gotanda, quoted from his presentation at the 6th Annual Conference of Asian and Pacific American Religion and Research Initiative (APARRI), Northwestern University, Evanston, Illinois, August 6, 2004.

another. Likewise, the democratization of America fought for by African and Asian Americans was advantageous for both groups.[38]

The question "Is Yellow Black or White?" reveals the complexity for Asian American racial identity and our place in society. "The question is only valid within the meanings given to and played out in the American racial formation, relations that have been posited as a black and white dyad," cautions David Kyuman Kim of Connecticut College.[39] Race as it is formed and expressed in the state of U.S. history, symbolic interactions, social structures of the society, as well as conflicts that arise out of both interactions and structures is highly complex. By posing the question of race in terms of a black and white dyad dismisses the gradations and complexities of the full spectrum between the racial poles and a larger question of the nature of American identity and racial formation. The navigating this complex situation of race as reflected in the question "Is Yellow Black or White" is the setting in which Asian Americans' claim for identity is also expressed. The term to describe this state of navigation is amphiboly as explained later in this work (Chapter 3). W. E. B. Du Bois talks about "two-ness" and "double-consciousness" to describe African Americans' soul and their view of the world.[40] For Asian Americans, our soul is translocal balancing a multiple set of consciousness. Translocality is multi-conscious among competing and contradictory ways of looking at reality. Translocality is Asian Americans' attempt to respond to the question of "Is Yellow Black or White," the question that leads to our contradictory and insurgent response to the way the question is posed. The translocality of Asian American racial identity also extends to the roles gender and sexuality play in both our self representations and imposed definitions of who we are. The heart of recognizing diversity within Asian Americans—gender, sexual, as well as national, generational, and class difference—is a particular notion of subjectivity. Lowe calls this diversity of Asian Americans as "hybridity, heterogeneity, and multiplicity."[41]

The notion of the subject as non-unitary, nomadic, and translocal stands in sharp contrast to the coherent and unitary identities that find expression in the recent discussions on diversity. Asian American femi-

---

38. Lowe, *Immigrant Acts*, 73.
39. Ibid., 75.
40. Du Bois, *The Souls of Black Folk*.
41. Lowe, *Immigrant Acts*.

nists and gay writers remind that subjectivity claim is often fraught with diffuse, shifting and often contradictory forces. Furthermore, the matter of sexuality for Asian Americans points to the state of marginalization of Asian Americans more acutely than any other forces that shape our identities. " . . . gay Asian organizations are not likely to view themselves as a gay subculture within Asian Americans any more than they are likely to think of themselves as an Asian American subculture within gay America," says Dona Takagi.[42] The marginalization is not as much about the quantities of experiences as it is about qualities of experience. "Identities whether sourced from sexual desire, racial origins, languages of gender, or class roots, are simply not additive," reminds Takagi.[43] Just as U.S. policies in Asia are interrelated with the construction of Asian Americans as a racial category, gender and sexuality are closely intertwined with the notion of race. Underlying much recent discussion about difference is the assumption that differences are comparable things. The notion that our differences are "separate but equal" is used to call attention to the specificity of experiences or to rally the troops under a collective banner. However, the "sameness" that underlies the difference between race and sexuality may be more fiction than fact. There are numerous ways that being "gay" is not like being "Asian." While both can be said to be socially constructed, being "gay" is performed and acted out, often individually, whereas being "Asian" is a "racial uniform" we wear and negotiated by political groups. "While it may seem politically efficacious to toss a gay or lesbian onto the diversity pile, adding one more form of subordination to the heap of inequalities, such as strategy glosses over the particular distinctive ways sexuality is troped in Asian America," says Dona Takagi.[44] What is at stake in each *different* identity category is the reality of human experiences which are diffuse, fluid, and often contradictory. A significant issue that arises out of these intersections is, once again, the dynamic ways we need to consider the *qualities* of our translocal experiences and multiple consciousnesses.

The question of who Asian Americans are is fraught with dubious assumptions and categories that need to be questioned. Scholars of Asian American studies affirm the articulation of "Asian American" identity while, at the same time, warning us of its generalizing and es-

42. Takagi, "Maiden Voyage" 1.
43. Ibid.
44. Ibid., 15.

sentializing dangers. But the one thing that can be said about Asian Americans is that lasting values and ideals of America emanate from underrepresented and disfranchised groups who occupy the margins of the society. Asian Americans play such a role in shaping these values and ideals. The contradictory and translocal self is the one who can question and the existing assumed values in our society, helps construct, joins conversations with other groups of citizens, and together imagines a healthy society that change history.

Throughout the history of the U.S., Asian Americans regularly engage in "racial identity play," an interactive negotiation process by which we Asian Americans confront and challenge the stereotypes and racial identities assigned to us. This negotiation has taken a multiple form—asserting ethnic uniqueness, dis-identifying with foreign appearances, taking advantage of ethnic identity capital, that is, the opportunities that accrue to us from others' perceptions, and the recent alliance of Asian Americans of northeast Asia descent with Americans of South Asia and Middle Eastern descent in the wake of the 9/11 incidents. This is to say that race structurally shapes group identities of Asian Americans and our individual and group opportunities, simultaneously forcing us and giving us a way of negotiating our beings in this society. This fluid and complex state of our existence has profound implications for the meaning of faith, value orientations, and morality for Asian Americans. Faith, may it be the monotheistic Judeo-Christian-Muslim faith or Tao, Hindu, or Buddhist faith, is not readily associated with certitude, permanence, stability, and exclusivity in this uncertain state of existence. Rather, faith for Asian Americans is intimately tied with ways of negotiating through this fluid, provisional, and translocal nature of life and still being able to savor the richness and joy of community and relationships. Faith for Asian Americans has to do with the power to sustain us in our continuing search for our identities in our racialized life. The driving force of such a faith is a new value orientation, or the morality of standing away from "home" in order to look at it with the provisional sense of detachment. Churches, temples, and other gathering places of worship and meditation are indeed the places that provide us the opportunities to ponder the question, what is it that attracts us to each other even in a highly racialized society that tends to divide people? based on these emerging religious and moral values.

RACE EXPERIENCE AS BEING "RUPTURALLY LIMINAL"

The translocality of Asian American experiences of race takes yet another expression, "ruptural liminality." It is the experience of life suddenly, without a warning, and rupturally disrupted by an outside force that has been the very source of trust. When disruption takes place, one is forced to negotiate the contradiction between the bewilderment of the betrayal of trust and one's desire to continue trusting the source of the betrayal. Ruptural liminality is akin to an experience of abuse inflicted by the trusted person, but in a societal scale. Dena Takagi points out that the "contradiction of nationalist identity formation is that it is precisely the demand for national cultural uniformity that inflicts differences with oppositional significance in antagonism to the apparatus whose function is to dictate that uniformity."[45] What happens when the demand for "national cultural uniformity" is suddenly disrupted and undermined? A sudden and ruptural injury gets inflicted on those who disrupt the demand just as in the case of sexual abuse. A powerful example of such an injury is the internment of Japanese Americans during World War II. Despite the U.S. government's own evidence that Japanese Americans posed no military threat, President Roosevelt signed Executive Order 9066, authorizing the removal and incarceration of 110,000 Japanese Americans. Two-thirds were American citizens and over half were children. Another example is the experiences of Arab and South Asian Americans following the 9/11. Jaideep Singh talks about the rupturally liminal experiences of the Sikh Americans.

> During the national hate crime epidemic that followed the attacks, Sikh Americans experienced domestic terrorism from their fellow citizens at the rate that exceeded that experienced by any other group in the country. Even as it became evident from the pictures of the hijackers and their suspected accomplices, that not one wore a turban, the attacks again Sikh Americans did not abate in any appreciable way for many weeks . . . When hate crimes were not being committed by bigots, they were being carried out legally by law enforcement officials. Racial profiling returned with a vengeance in the wake of the terrorist attacks, and most Americans—sadly even many African Americans and

---

45. Ibid., 17.

Latinos, who know firsthand the injuries caused by this heinous policy—were reported to be in favor of it.[46]

Ruptural liminality is a way of living with the unresolvedness of tragedy and woundedness that unexpectedly and thus rupturally intrudes into otherwise stable and tranquil life. Rupturally liminal experiences inflicted upon Asian Americans are so insidious because they are "indicative of the type of utter disdain and disrespect accorded to Muslims by high ranking leaders in Western nations, a disregard mirrored by far too many politicians and media outlets in the United States," says Singh in reference to the post 9/11 experiences of Sikh Americans.[47] Targeted American citizens, may they be Japanese Americans during World War II or Arab and South Asian Americans following 9/11, were identified for incarceration or attack by their racial characteristics, their appearances. In many cases, the visible markers which distinguished the victims were actually religious signifiers as in the case of Sikh and Arab Americans. In this regard,

> These religious symbols become racialized in the eyes of what Bill Ong Hing calls the "vigilante racist" carrying out these assaults.... In essence, they found themselves facing a new form of American apartheid, one which has been operating since the fall of 2001.[48]

At the same time, Asian Americans claim the legitimacy of tragedy and woundedness that are often not acknowledged by the mass institutions. In order to counter the forces of national cultural uniformity, insurgent and subversive narratives are emerging among Asian American communities. If translocality characterizes the experiences of race for Asian Americans, the value orientations and "morality" that emerge out of our racial translocality is nomadic and "ruptually liminal." The translocal character of race for Asian Americans is at the same time "ruptural" because Americans' racial identities are tied with the very social structure of this nation as Omi and Winant describe it in their book *Racial Formation in the United States*. The state which is the architect of segregation and the main enforcer of racial difference tends to reproduce the patterns of inequality in a new guise. As a result, certain

---

46. Singh, "Sikhs and 9/11," 1–2.
47. Singh "9/11 & 7/7," 11.
48. Ibid., 1.

racialized groups of people are subject to discriminately practice by the policy decisions made by the state through its various apparatuses. From the Chinese exclusion act of 1882 to the internment of Japanese Americans during World War II, and the unauthorized surveillance of Americans of southern Asian descent following the 9/11 have been ruptural in the experiences of Asian Americans. The sense of security and stability of life are abruptly disrupted by the particular policy decisions made by the state. The words of Joseph E. Lowery, then president of the Southern Christian Leadership Conference, on the occasion of the twenty years commemoration of the march from Selma to Montgomery in 1985 speaks of the ruptural life of many racialized people in the U.S. "We have kept the faith but the nation has not kept its promise." In the history of the U.S. political forces have attempted so many times to turn back the clock of racial history. There is no stability to be counted on in the lives of racially minoritized people. Asian Americans are no exception. Our peaceful and stable lives can be taken away anytime. Those Asian Americans who experienced the assaults from the very source of their trust in democracy, Americans and the American government, responded in very heroic ways. The stories of Japanese Americans and their roles in the 442 Regimental Combat Team in the European theater during World War II are well known. The 442nd was a self-sufficient fighting force, and fought with uncommon distinction in Italy, southern France and Germany. The unit became the most highly decorated military unit in the history of the United States Armed Forces. While the so-called "No No Boys" demonstrated their own dignity and pride by an act of civil disobedience that sent the draft eligible Japanese American men to prison while others chose to volunteer or be drafted into the U.S. Army out of their internment camps and fight overseas.

Following the racist treatments incurred on Arab and South Asian Americans, they came together united to get the message out that they were being attacked, and that they were not going to endure this assault in silence. This time was characterized by a remarkable rise of grass roots activism throughout their communities.

> Across the nation, formerly politically inert Sikh Americans vaulted into action. From those operating at ground zero mobilizing Sikh taxi drivers to provide free rides to volunteers in the rescue effort and family members searching for news of loved ones in involved in the tragedy, to a young Sikh American surgi-

cal resident who—at risk of life and limb—rushed to the scene of the disaster and helped set up and work the first triage station established at ground zero, just in front of one of the collapsed towers, Sikh American activists in New York City led the way for Sikhs across the country. At the vanguard of the activism are second-generation, young, Sikh professionals and college students.[49]

Being caught between the unjust racialized treatment rupturally inflicted on Asian Americans by the very society and the government that they come to trust, Asian Americans historically have embodied the meaning of democratic freedom by their own sacrificial acts. Asian Americans experience race as liminal in value orientation. Race is a way of living with the unresolvedness of historical injuries and, at the same time, claiming the legitimacy of an alternative to the mass institutions that do not acknowledge the impact of the woundedness. A rupturally liminal race is not a matter of choice. One is either born into this state of life or finds oneself in this state one day and refuses to sit on the sidelines. A person living in the state of ruptural liminality cultivates a scrupulous subjectivity. Such a person knows that in a changing world an identity is always provisional. Borders and barriers that enclose us within the safety of familiar territory can also become prisons and often defended beyond reason or necessity. Loss and transience are inherent in the very existence as a "People on the Way." Ruptural liminality is the new way of forging Asian American identity that provides a clue to an alternate vision of bringing people together within the current state of the American racial scene.

PANETHNICITY

A traditional paradigm in race relations is to treat each Asian American ethnic group linearly and as a separate and relatively homogenous entity. This paradigm results in descriptions of ethnic-specific experiences that are circumscribed, while assumed to be representative of the entire community. Consequently, policy recommendations that address the needs of a particular Asian American ethnic group or Asian Americans in general presume a one-size-fits-all solution that does not meet the range and

---

49. Singh, "Sikhs and 9/11," 20.

complexity of contemporary communities. The emerging paradigm, on the other hand, recognizes the "heterogeneity, multiplicy, and hybridity" of Asian America and of each Asian American group. Conventionally understood, a commonly held belief system and culture brings people together as a community. Yen Le Espiritu argues that an imposed notion of identity from outside such as the term "Orientals" serves as an opportunity for creating a community coherence of our own. No longer separated by old world political conflicts, languages, and customs, Asian Americans can see the political necessity and social advantages of uniting and speaking with one voice. "While ethnicity may be an exercise of personal choice of Euro-Americans, it is not so for nonwhite groups in the United States."[50] Culture is usually understood as a means to delineate a boundary. But, culture is also the product of a boundary.

> Hence, objective cultural differences need to be distinguished from the socially constructed boundaries that ultimately define ethnic groups. When this potential is taken up and mobilized, a cultural group, a group of people who share an identifiable set of meanings, symbols, values, and norms, is transformed into an ethnic group, one with a conscious group identity.[51]

Panethnic self-identification of Asian Americans is forged primarily through the symbolic re-interpretation of our shared history, particularly when this history involves racial subjugation. "[P]anethnic entrepreneurs mobilize around symbolic group boundaries and strategically construct who belongs to the group," says sociologist Russell Jeung.[52] Even though panethnic group identity is circumstantially constructed, it is not necessarily circumstantially maintained. Once established, increasing interaction among its members result in a commonly shared values and group consciousness, common interpretations of their experiences and those of the larger society. "Culture building is essential in consolidating ethnic boundaries because it promotes group consciousness, reminding members constantly of disproportionate importance of what they shared, in comparison to what they did not."[53]

---

50. Espiritu, *Asian American Panethnicity*, 6.
51. Ibid., 9.
52. Jeung, *Faithful Generations*, 14.
53. Ibid., 12.

This emerging new paradigm recognizes heterogeneity within the group and the role of social class, gender, ethnicity, sexual orientation, the perspectives and experiences of different generations, political and economic dynamics, specific historical situations, political affiliations, regionality, and other dimensions that challenge the limitations of the existing homogeneous ethnic-specific paradigm. How to negotiate these differences that exist within the panethnic identity of Asian Americans and still maintain its group coherence is a real challenge. If Asian Americans are to build a self-consciously pan-Asian solidarity, they need to take seriously the heterogeneities among their ranks and overcome the narrow dominance of one class or that of the two oldest Asian American groups. This task of "bridging" reminds us that ethnicization, the process of boundary construction, is not only reactive, a response to pressures from the external environment, but also creative, a product of internally generated dynamics.[54]

Hybridity is Lisa Lowe's response to the challenge posed by the emergence of the panethnic identity of Asian Americans. Rooted in the cultural studies of such figures as Homi Bhabha and Stewart Hall, her definition of hybridity also provides an important clue for the construction of religious articulation of faith for Asian Americans as noted in the chapter three. Hybridity, according to Lowe, is "the formation of cultural objects and practices that are produced by the histories of uneven and unsynthetic power relations: for example, the racial and linguistic mixings in the Philippines and among Filipinos in the United States are the material trace of the history of Spanish colonialism, U.S. colonization, and U.S. neocolonialism."[55] Hybridity produces a previously unexpected outcome out of such a relationship of power disparity. In other words, it creates a new world that is previously unknown and unknowable. It cannot be equated with assimilation of Asian or immigrant practices to dominant forms. Rather, it "marks the history of survival within relationships of unequal power and domination."[56] Combined with "heterogeneity," "the existence of differences and differential relationships within a bounded category," and "multiplicity," "the ways in which subjects located within social relations are determined by several different axes of power, are multiply determined by the contradictions of capitalism,

---

54. Ibid, 176.
55. Lowe, *Immigrant Acts*, 16.
56. Ibid.

patriarchy, and race relations," the hybridization of Asian Americans as its emerging identity is a description of the uneven process through which we encounter the violences of racial formation and racism and the process through which we survive those violences by living, inventing, and reproducing different cultural alternatives."[57]

The hybridization as a powerful Asian American identity takes place within our efforts for our own self-representation through an institution-building. Asian American studies is indeed about institution-building, both within and outside the Asian American community, of our struggle for our right to interpret the reality we shared with the majority through the institutions we create or infiltrate. This is also the case for Asian American religious and theological studies. Increasingly, Asian American religious and theological studies focus on the future of current religious institutions rather than religion per se, and on the changing ways in which believers ¾ or seekers ¾ related their personal faith to the public engagements. In such institutions an alternate approach to inquiry takes place. Yen Le Espiritu, for example, proposes an alternative to the structural/discursive debate by placing at the center of inquiry the interconnected relations and complexity of the Asian American experience itself rather than the supposed two poles of the debate.[58] In the exploration of how Asian American family relations, labor experiences, and systems of meaning are affected by racism, class exploitation and patriarchy, Espiritu utilizes an interdisciplinary approach that brings together sociology, history, ethnic studies, anthropology, literature, critical legal studies, and cultural studies. Espiritu points to the opportunities for transforming the existing structures by forging cross-gender, cross-racial, cross-class alliances rather than remain in the double or triple burden of intertwined gender, race and class oppression. Neil Gotanda also proposes a narrative articulation of contradiction by approaching religion from the perspective of the "racialization of religion."[59] According to Gotanda, religion in the eye of the dominant culture sometimes plays the role of being perceived as foreign and hostile. In the aftermath of the September 11, 2001, Islam in

---

57. Ibid., 82.
58. Espiritu, *Asian American Women and Men*.
59. Gotanda, his presentation on "Racialization of Religion" in the 2002 APARRI Conference (Asian Americans, Religion, and Research Initiative, sponsored by PANA Institute, Pacific School of Religion, Berkeley, California).

particular has become equated with certain racial groups, i.e., people of Middle Eastern, South Asia, and Southeast Asia descent, thereby, creating a degree of suspicion and hostility against them. The foreignness of religions is expressed in a racialized perception of their adherents. Religion becomes racialized. The question Gotanda poses is the ways of disclaiming the imposed racialized reading of religions and to provide a counter understanding of Asian American religions.

RACIALIZED FAITH

Asian American communities are fragile, nomadic, and often lacking in stability. We are constantly "on the way." A primary reason for the lack of stability is the way the Asian American racial identities are forged and lived. Race is not just a category to classify us in the American racial hierarchy. Race points to a particular way Asian Americans live our translocal, nomadic, unstable, hybrid, and a shifting identity that is often ruptured and changed without much of a prior warning. To summarize what race is all about for Asian Americans, race is historically tied with the U.S. foreign policies. It is also internally "Orientalized" within the very communities in which Asian American situate ourselves. Race is contradicted between the image of "model minority" and "foreigners within." It intrudes as rupturally liminal experiences, and politically organized as pan-ethnic identity. Race is a complex sum of these different experiences. Race is indeed the "continuing contradiction." It is the site for alternative histories and memories that provides the grounds to imagine who we are as Asian Americans. "Reclaiming a voice in this context has also been about reclaiming, reconnecting and reordering those ways of knowing which were submerged, hidden or driven underground."[60] Asian Americans are indeed "People on the Way."

In order to consider the significance of our translocal and rupturally liminal experiences of race for the shaping of Asian Americans' second language, we will need to consider the religious and moral dimensions of translocality and ruptural liminality. Asian Americans 'faith practice is intrinsically entwined with this translocal and rupturally liminal character of our race experiences. Our faith practice is a reflective endeavor that is intertwined with a story about the shaping of Asian Americans'

---

60. Smith, *Decolonizing Methodologies*, 69.

translocally and rupturally liminally racialized experiences, values, and life orientations. Correspondingly, our faith practice operates within an alternate set of religious and moral value formulations both within and outside the Asian American community, and of our struggle for a right to interpret the reality we share with other racialized groups of Americans through the institutions we infiltrate. In the process, we cultivate the posture of standing "away from 'home' in order to look at it with the exile's detachment."[61] In other words, Asian Americans are "not being at home in [our] own home." This translocal value orientation provides us Asian Americans an angle of vision to see the world with our own nomadic translocality of souls, the nomadic translocality that may well be the common experience that brings people of disparate backgrounds together. Religious discourse is an articulation of what it means to be Asian Americans as translocal "disorienting subjects" through the lens of faith.[62] That is the reason why "faith" is an integral aspect of Asian American lives. Religious discourse for Asian Americans is indeed a "performative scholarship," allowing us to "project [our own] structures onto the theoretical approach" as a way to introduce fresh ways of viewing life.[63] Religious discourse thus takes on a politically and culturally insurgent character of de-legitimating the national myth embedded in the America's first tongue about what it means to be an American and re-inscribing what life can be even under the current circumstances of domination and restrictive freedom.

Christian faith-thinking, for example, does this domination and restrictive freedom through the lens of Christian communities' historically formed narratives that are originated in the Mediterranean and North Atlantic context as they are reinterpreted and re-inscribed within the Asian American material life of its racialized history. In other words, "Christian theology" for Asian American Christians has to do with the task of reclaiming, reconnecting and reordering those ways of knowing which were submerged, hidden or driven underground in Asian American experiences. In such a re-inscription, the translocaity of Asian American racialized identities refer to a disruptive fashion in which one's value-orientation emerges against the value orientation,

61. Ibid., 185.
62. Busto, "Disorienting Subjects," 9–28.
63. Ibid., 24. Rudy Busto here quotes Buddhist scholar Bernard Faure, *Chan Insights and Oversights*, 151.

the first tongue, prevalent in our society. Our translocality affirms the emergence of a new world in which Asian Americans together with the rest of the Americans inhabit in a fresh and different way from what we have experienced before. Theology is as yet one among many endeavors by Asian Americans to claim our own translocal identities in a society whose propensity is to erase such claims in the name of national unity and the assimilation of differences.

W. E. B. Du Bois's notion of the "veil" is instructive in describing this notion of hope in America. The "veil," too, is the locus of religious efforts of Asian Americans through a different mirror.[64] The veil of oppression necessitates a double consciousness that exists behind the veil, the color line for people of color, says Du Bois. This other consciousness remains opaque to the dominant racial community because of the singularity of its perspective. This opacity behind the veil extends to the language, culture, historical memory of people of color and the way life is narrated by them. An assertion of the individual and communal subjectivity of those who exist behind the veil is a means by which the opaque veil is contained and the historicity of official narratives exposed through re-inscription. Such an assertion often takes place in the form of institution-building by people behind the veil. Asian American faith communities are a part of the American religious experience that has not been adequately considered. Our faith communities are, to a large measure, a product of the refusal of the racially dominant group to accept us Asian Americans as "an equal before God" and an equal with the people of the dominant group. Our faith communities, may they be a Christian church or a Buddhist temple, is a product of our desire to shape our own destiny, to exercise our freedom, and uphold the democracy by creating our own institutions.

Once again, Asian Americans' reading of our racialized material life is both contradictory and insurgent in character, contradictory to the prevailing dominant reading of history and insurgent in exposing the limit of the dominant racial group's reading of life. Christian theology, for example, is historically formed within myriad societal and cultural contexts. In the theological discourse, "historicism," as Ernst Troeltsch named it, has been traditionally understood to be the locus of theologizing as H. Richard Niebuhr pointed out some decades ago. "It remains true that Christian faith cannot escape from partnership with

---

64. Du Bois, *Souls of Black Folks*.

history, however many other partners it may choose. With this it has been mated and to this its loyalty belongs; the union is as indestructible as that of reason and sense experience in the natural sciences."[65] In other words, Niebuhr argues that our reflective and interpretive endeavors are conditioned by socio-historical location and context in which "history" is defined. However, historicism, *historisums* in Troeltschian terms, or historical consciousness, is not value neutral. It is politically charged, culturally conditioned, and racially prescribed. The questions of whose stories are told and listened to, who participates in the shaping of a tradition, and who determines the validity of a story, are fraught with the pain of the veil borne by those who have been historically excluded from its subjectivity claim and self-representation. Even the popular assumption about narratives that says that narratives overcome historical discontinuities to create coherent or continuous wholes is questionable. If certain narratives disrupt continuity and coherence, what happens then? Niebuhr did caution us by saying that "When we speak of revelation in the Christian church we refer to *our* history, to the history of selves or to history as it is lived and apprehended from within."[66] Niebuhr talks about "our history." Who are "us"? What Niebuhr failed to address is the different ways in which the meaning of revelation are *historically* understood and experienced in a racialized world and by racialized Christians. Who are talking about "*our* history?" The commonality of the meaning of revelation is not necessarily assumed among racialized communities. Narratives of identity and racial formations told by Asian Americans de-legitimize the notion of equivalency of differences and re-inscribe the otherness of simultaneous identities, reminding us Asian Americans once again our translocality and ruptrul liminality which is never fully commensurable among the differences.[67]

For those who live behind the veil often have a distinct experience of revelation that could disrupt the continuity of the traditionally interpreted meaning of the divine disclosure in the North Atlantic history. The translocality for Asian American Christians is sometimes expressed in terms of "amphibolous" reading and even questioning, for example, of the once-and-for-all-ness of the divine revelation in the person of Jesus

---

65. Niebuhr, *The Meaning of Revelation*, 43.

66. Ibid., 44.

67. Althusser, "Contradiction and Overdetermination," 99; and Hall, "Signification, Representation, Ideology," 91–114.

of Nazareth. This is so because of our racialized readings of the meaning of revelation. The decisiveness and absoluteness of revelation based on the cosmological foundation of radical monotheism is suspect for Asian Americans because of its racialized meaning of superiority and exclusion of others. For Asian Americans, the religious epistemological foundation is not necessarily monotheism, rather it is likely to be non-theistic or multitheistic. This is the insight that is not fully appreciated in the current theological discourse. In other words, the very monotheistic assumption brought into the current theological discourse on Christian faith does not allow a room for a more nuanced multivalency of faith experiences and multiple religious belongings of Asian Americans. This is so because an acceptance of multiplicity and ambiguity of faith experiences and religious and cosmological belongings expose the assumed foundation of Christian faith as it has been historically defined in the western context and thus disrupt the ongoing theological conversation with Asian Americans. The conversation becomes too threatening for those who are not conscious of the veil. Asian Americans' theological discourse is insurgent rooted in its challenge of the historically assumed epistemological and cosmological basis of Christian monotheistic faith. This matter will be taken up again in the third chapter.

What is happening in the narrative descriptions of Asian Americans is a way in which historicism is re-articulated and re-inscribed not in terms of individuation, equivalence, or pluralism, "but out of contradiction as a site for alterative histories and memories that provide the grounds to imagine subject, community, and practice in new ways."[68] The "contradiction as a site" is neither monolithic nor fixed. It is spaces of continuing struggles between the historically prescribed ideological imperative for equivalence out of individuation on the one hand and, on the other, counter acts of dissent and refusal that are always in the process of speaking out of one's subjectivity and speaking against ideologies of identification. These spaces of contradiction, discordance, and sometimes of enmity are the locus of religious and theological discourse for Asian Americans. In these spaces, the Christian notion of revelation, for example, is narrated as a particularly noted event in history, which, at times, validates Asian American claims for subjectivity or, at other times, reminds us of the stifling historicity and power of the "traditioned" narratives of Christian faith which have delegitimized and dismissed our

---

68. Lowe, *Immigrant Acts*, 96.

faith claims. The "meaning of revelation" is often enigmatic and "amphibolous" in character for Asian Americans as this term is addressed in the third chapter. Revelation is not readily viewed as the decisive paradigmatic event in history that fashions the people of Christian faith into the future that was already anticipated in the past narratives as H. Richard Niebuhr claimed. Revelation bears more the character of perplexity, the absence of certitude, ambivalence, co-existence of contradictory worldviews, "amphiboly," that lead us, Asian Americans, to silence rather than being the measure of a clearly articulated life definition and the stable signal of the promised humanity.

And the main cause of such ambivalence about revelation has to do with the racialized reading of the Christian faith by Asian Americans, particularly the act of questioning the claimed superiority of the racially dominant Anglo European group for their equation of the U.S. with the biblical notion of the "Chosen People." Andre Siegfried's judgment that Protestantism is historically understood as America's "only national religion and to ignore that fact is to view the country from a false angle" is the context of the troublesome meaning of the "Chosen People" for Asian Americans[69] H. Richard Niebuhr in his classic *The Kingdom of God in America* traced that impact of Protestantism in a still another way. Puritans search for assurance of election and their desire for a purified church membership gradually led them to the view that an inward (subjective) experience of God's grace was an essential mark of a Christian. What emerges among Asian American Christians is a new conception of Christian piety, ruptural hybridity and liminality, that would in due course have profound but disruptive effects on religion, social behavior, and church order throughout the Protestant world, and particularly in the New World.

Lin Chi Wang of the University of California, Berkeley argues that the white supremacy in the U.S. is directly linked to this theological concept of the Chosen People as this theological concept was appropriated by Puritans and serves as the theological foundation of the Declaration of Independence and the Bill of Rights.[70] Historically, by 1776 Jonathan Edwards's notion that the Kingdom of God was commencing in America had been translated by the authors of the Declaration of Independence into an official dogma: that heaven smiled upon the new nation, making

69. Siegfried is quoted by Niebuhr, *The Kingdom of God in America*, 17.
70. Wang, "White Supremacy and the Bible."

it a "new order of the ages" (*e pluribus unum . . . annuity coeptis . . . novus ordo seclorum.*) Jefferson, Adams, and Franklin would agree that as Israel of old had been led through the wilderness to the Promised Land, so also had the United States become God's New Israel. The exclusivity of Christian faith thus is intimately related to the historically racialized American life. The very foundational theological assumption that support this society need sto be questioned, says Wang. The notion of the divine chosenness associated with the national values raises the red flag for those who have been excluded from the historically chosen circle of existence. In their readings of American life a reformation of the existing s societal values cannot be attained, for how can one restore that which has not been established, i.e., a true equal and just society, when the nation was founded on the basis of exclusion of certain segments of the society? And yet, the reality of the history and current state of the society cannot be reversed either. This nation has been firmly built on the premise of what Thomas Jefferson called "of that Being in whose hands we are, who led our forefathers, as Israel of old, from their native land and planted them in a country flowing with all the necessaries and comforts of life, who had covered our infancy with his providence and our riper years with his wisdom and power."[71] People of color exist in this interstitial space of the historical reality of the exclusive societal structure on the one hand, our own yearnings for an alternate structuring of our society with an equal representation of our own historical experiences, on the other. This interstice in which Asian Americans find ourselves is the amphibolous state of our existence. In this interstice the faith posture arises as the way of coping with the vexing life.

This is to say that for Asian Americans the determinative locus of religious and theological reflections is located in the sociohistorical racial formation in the U.S., the ways we have been racially prescribed and classifies. For Asian Americans, faith talk has to do with our own efforts to construct institutions and spaces to create cultural alternatives and subjectivity by our own narrative inscriptions. These motivating forces provide the impetus for faith reflection within Asian American communities. Talk about faith is an attempt among a milliard of attempts to narrate the story of events that shape the historical formation of our racial identities. Narration of the racial formation is standpoint specific. It is the work of the present that exists under the "veil" seeking to un-

---

71. Berocovitch, *The Puritan Origins of the American Self,* 139.

derstand the past that was also lived behind the "veil" that still covers us. Our racialized faith narratives seek to connect with those who preceded us in the past, and to establish us the continuity of identity with those who lived in history, indicating that our own present situation, though different in some sense, is also similar in other ways. Such narratives of identity and subjectivity-claim reverberate between Asian Americans of the present and the past that is full of meaning. Religious narratives told in this locus are necessarily politicized and subversive in character, for we Asian Americans engage in historical re-interpretation and de-legitimization of the officially sanctioned narratives and also participate in historical transformation of the reigning tradition, whether be it secular or religious. In this sense, Asian American religious and theological articulation is a narrative of "subaltern" communities whose histories are fragmented, episodic, and identifiable most likely from a point of historical hindsight or through the "veil" that is our translocal existence that forges a new way of imagining the architecture of the American society and a world.

In summary, translocality and ruptural liminality describe the link between the state of racial reality as a "contradictory site" and the meaning of Asian American identity that arises out of this site. Translocality is the term that describes the lives and identities of those whose lives are not stable, certain, and predictable. It describes "People on the Way." Translocality is, at the same time, a nomadic and provisional life-orientation due in part to Asian Americans' rupturally liminal experiences. These two terms point to a site for an alternate reading of history, identity, and memory based on a constantly shifting racial identity of Asian Americans amidst this contradictory site of race in the U.S. The value orientation and morality claimed by those who embrace translocality and ruptural liminality are those emerging out of the "morality not to be at home in one's home."[72] Culturally translocality and ruptural liminaity are also expressed in such Asian American literature as *Dictee* and Asian American rap, *King Giddra*, which make explicit that unvalued social formation includes a multiplicity of social contradictions—of, race, national origin, ethnicity, gender, or class. Translocality privileges heterogeneous origins and conditions, with certain contradictions taking priority over others at particular historical moments. Asian Americans' faith practice is intrinsically entwined with translocality and ruptural

72. Adorno quoted by Said in *Reflections on Exile and Other Essays*, 184.

liminality. Faith narratives are articulated at an intersection with both descriptive and prescriptive determinations; each demands different repetitions of the faith, and each is inextricably implicated in the forms of fidelity demanded by the others. Our faith practice is a reflective endeavor that is intertwined with a story about the shaping of Asian American racial identity. Correspondingly, our faith practice operates within an alternate set of value formation both within and outside the Asian American community, of our struggle for a right to interpret the reality we share with other racialized groups of Americans through the institutions we infiltrate. In the process, we cultivate that "morality" to "stand away from 'home' in order to look at it with the outsider's detachment."[73] This morality provides us Asian Americans an angle of vision to see the world with its own woundedness of souls, the woundedness that may well be the common experience that brings people of disparate backgrounds together. This issue is treated in the second chapter more precisely under the subject of pathos as another necessary scaffold for the context of our theological endeavor. In a similar token, amphibolous perceptions of our racial classification juxtaposed with a history of migration, cultural interaction, oppression, and exploitation as well as parallel and mutual struggles for freedom out of our shared history and memory of a kindred people, set the locus of faith reflection for Asian Americans (Chapter Three). Along with the Asian American experiences as translocal and rupturally liminal person, race "clarifies the existential predicament of Asian Americans, [and provides] a deeper understanding of the cultural, political, social, and economic contexts of Asian American religious practices."[74] Asian American scholars of religion highlight the primacy of race in the development of our faith communities. Jane Iwamura of University of Southern California observes:

> At the most basic level, "Asian American/Pacific Islander" (API) serves as a salient marker of [racial] identity in the U.S. This racial category creates a space at the multicultural table for previously ignored, underrepresented points of view. The inclusion of the religious experience of Asian American communities and individuals thus broadens and enriches our general understanding of American religion.[75]

---

73. Ibid., 185.
74. Kim, "Enchanting Diasporas," 327.
75. Iwamura and Spickard, eds., *Revealing the Sacred in Asian & Pacific America*, 2.

Theologian Sang Hyun Lee notes Asian Americans' sense of marginality that is created by racial barriers and calls on Asian American churches and theology to "affirm its ethnic particularity against racism."[76] Theology for Asian Americans is both a racialized and politicized endeavor carved out of our responses to the way the racial formation of Asian Americans is constructed. Faith talks, Christian or otherwise, carried out amidst the amphibolous perceptions of Asian Americans' racial classification are less monological, doctrinal, and responsive to a particular determinative singular historical occurrence. Asian American faith talks are dialogical, participatory, and responsive to a multiplicity of historical occurrences which are often contradictory one with another, when viewed out of our own discordant experiences as its sources. Faith talk in such a locus does not allow the luxury of resolution and certitude. It is more tolerant of ambiguity and questioning. The centrality of revelation as assumed in the institutionalized traditioned reading of Christian faith is yet a confirmation of these discordant experiences of ours out of our racialized experiences in the U.S. In other words, the centrality and primacy of revelation remind in the historicized Christian theology remind us of the white supremacy by which norm race is constructed in this society. Institutionalized patterns of interpretation, may it be a creedal confession of faith or a widely accepted theological and doctrinal formulation, are implicitly or explicitly functionalist and administrative but also racialized. They purport to show how culturally or racially dominant systems of meaning are stabilized and reproduced over time. As a result, such analyses often screen out "deviant" events like micro and macro-political resistances and conflicts. The racial formation of Asian Americans expose such functionalist and instrumental methodologies, whether in social sciences or in theology, for when they are applied to race issues, these methods occult Asian American subjectivity and construe us as either invisible or, at best, passive victims of racial domination by another group. In order to counter such tendency both in the past and the present, a faith articulation of the life of Asian Americans through the lens of our faith communities are necessarily situated in a broader, non-functionalist perspective for the reading of our racialized life.

76. Lee, "Pilgrimage and Home in the Wilderness of Marginality," 244–53.

BRAKING THE TRADITION

> I want to break tradition – unlock this room
> Where women dress in the dark.
> Discover the lies my mother told me.
> the lies that we are small and powerless
> that our possibilities must be compressed
> to the size of pearls, displayed only as
> passive chokers, charms around our neck.
> Break Tradition.
> I want to tell my daughter of this room
> of myself
> filled with tears of shakuhachi.
> . . . .
> poems about madness,
> sounds shaken from barbed wire and
> goodbyes and miracles of survival.
> This room of open window where daring ones escape.
> My daughter denies she is like me . . .
> her pouting ruby lips, her skirts
> swaying to salsa, teena marie and the stoners,
> her thighs displayed in carnivals of color.
> I do not know the contents of her room.
> She mirrors my aging,
> She is breaking tradition.[77]

Asian Americans speak of translocal dislocation, nomadically ruptural and liminal life experiences, amphibolous faith and life orientation, unresolvedness of contradictions, and silence, amidst the assumed dominant cultural and cosmological values of the society thereby transgressing these prevailing publically accepted values. "Ultimately, revealing is always hiding; any insight generates its own blindness; any deconstruction is always already a reconstruction," says Faure.[78] Contradictions embedded in translocality and ruptural liminality are not readily resolved but are seen as the very source of life's vitality and the very texture of life understanding as much as of pain and lament.

---

77. Mirikitani, 9. "Breaking Tradition", from SHEDDING SILENCE: POETRY AND PROSE by Janice Mirikitani, copyright © 1987 by Janice Mirikitani. Used by permission of Celestial Arts, an imprint of the Crown Publishing Group, a division of Random House, Inc.

78. Faure, *Chan Insights and Oversights*, 151.

"Breaking tradition" is another way of coming to term with the translocal and rupturally liminal woundedness of our own racialized history of contradiction amidst American success culture that is rich in optimism. *Annuit coeptis:* God has blessed our beginnings so says the seal on the dollar bill. But Asian American experiences are fraught with the denial of reasons for optimism at this crucial juncture in American history. Asian Americans can take the measure of the cramping boundaries of existence—and still affirm. This is perhaps a value that will be needed in the America's future, since we as people have run out of space and our nation is increasingly cramped so far as assertiveness and success in world affairs are concerned. When the tragic sense is acknowledged in American civic and religious life, as in Abraham Lincoln and in the aftermath of 9/11, the world has listened to us Americans. In the course of history the racialized Americans, Asian Americans and numerous other racially and culturally disfranchised people in our own cultural and storied sites have developed our own perspectives and readings of the tragic history of the nation through a "different mirror." We Asian Americans know that America is a cultural site where the images of both "yellow perils" and "exotic perpetual foreigners" were created. Not only the image of the exotic Asia, the Orient, America has helped shape an oppositional pattern of relationship across racial lines in the U.S., thereby creating a distinct identity of America discrediting those who hold an alternate reading of history through a "different mirror." The racialized "different mirror" intersects with the ways Asian other disfranchised Americans have come together to establish the communities of our own in order to create the "space" of our own. Race is also reflected in the development of Asian and other Americans of color our own religious communities, the communities where the meaning of translocality and ruptural liminality is identified, reflected, and cherished as our quest for faith understanding. Faith and race are inseparably linked in America.

Hybridization, cross-gender, cross-racial, cross-class alliances, and counter racialized understanding of religion are indicators of subjectivity that is deeply connected between political agency and social identity. The "continuing contradiction as a site for alterative histories and memories that provide the grounds to imagine subject, community, and practice in new ways" shapes Asian American subjectivity in a new light. "Reclaiming a voice in this context has also been about reclaiming, reconnecting and reordering those ways of knowing which were submerged, hidden or driven underground."⁷⁹ Memory of the past, way of knowing, historical agency and political priorities are intimately connected in the formation of subjectivity. As Homi Bhabha reminds us: "how does the intellectual affiliate with political priorities that are to be found in the act of articulating, or contesting, differential political objectives—feminism, anti-racism, homophobia—rather than in the 'objects' of difference themselves?"⁸⁰ The question, religious or otherwise, is this: "How are subjects formed 'in-between' or in excess of, the sum of the parts of difference (usually intoned as race/class/gender/etc.)?"⁸¹

Break Tradition. This is one of the responses to this question. A potent locus of breaking the monolithic and singular tradition is the intersection of a unified national identity and its resultant paradoxical exposure of the silenced pain of Asian American narratives of our own subjectivity claims. This intersection creates an opportunity for us to refute the myth of the official narratives of race and re-articulate an alternate reading of representational democratization of the society by living, inventing, and reproducing different cultural alternatives. "Analyzing the symbolic nature of race helps explain how Asian American faith communities have been established and the diverse subcultures that result. The power of these symbolic racial identities draw people together, as well as keep people apart," comments sociologist Russell Jeung.⁸² The efforts to reinvent a cultural alternative take many forms. One such an example is Asian American evangelical parachurch groups. The stereotypical "model minority" perception of Asian Americans, particularly Asian American evangelical students, induces what Rudy Busto of University of California, Santa Barbara terms, "double whammy" effect of race and religion for them. " . . . evangelical parachurch groups may become safe havens against both racial antagonism and secular systems of thought," prompting an alternative identity based not on race or ethnicity, but on faith.⁸³ This is an example of re-articulation. Religious and racial identities intersect and become integrated rather than competing for Asian Americans. Contrary to evangelical and mainline Protestant churches of the Anglo European population, Asian

---

79. Smith, *Decolonizing Methodologies*, 69.
80. Bhabha, "Frontlines/Borderposts," 272.
81. Ibid., 269.
82. Jeung, *Faithful Generations*, 159.
83. Busto, "The Gospel according to the Model Minority?" 180.

American evangelicals understand their communities as a network of people with similar family socialization patterns and lifestyle affinities. These evangelical groups share the mainstream evangelical values, but "its Asian American identity is symbolically important; the effective leaders represent authentic, strong Christians who are Asian American as well."[84] The symbolization of Asian American evangelicals takes on different expressions. The primary symbol is and remains to be race and its impact upon Asian Americans. On the other hand, both mainline and evangelical Protestants view Asian Americans as "a disenfranchised people of color who need to reclaim their ethnic heritage."[85]

Asian American women are also claiming the need for breaking tradition and "re-centering" them in the predominantly male-oriented readings of our racial identities.[86] This effort is a particularly thorny issue because of the demographics of Asian women's migration to the United States. They were not present in the early stage of the Asian migration to the U.S. Their voices were not well represented due largely to the patriarchal cultures that the Asian American communities inherited from Asia. Asian American women's efforts for re-centering thus highlight the loosening of patriarchy's grip. At the same time, Asian American women also live in a radicalized society. "Is it possible," Okihiro poses the question, "in passing on Asian culture to the next generation, 'Americanized' (not in its usual meaning of assimilation or Anglo-conformity, but in the sense of transformation and democratization) that culture by subverting its patriarchal forms and meanings and thereby helped to liberate themselves?"[87] In both the institution-buildings of Asian American faith communities and Asian American women's claim for "re-centering," Asian American racial identity is symbolic in character based on culture or concrete material interests. What is at stake is the self-definition, self-representation and narrative understandings of our own that will contribute to the future of American peoplehood.

---

84. Jeung, *Faithful Generations*, 160.
85. Ibid.
86. Okihiro, *Margins and Mainstreams*, 64–92.
87. Ibid., 92.

3

The Spirit of Dissonance and Dissent

DIASPORIC ASIAN AMERICA

"THE PHYSICAL LOCATION OF the unknown, a sense that it is elsewhere, is an aspect of the mystery of knowledge that is often forgotten when we have overcome our ignorance . . . Knowing is a secure place to be," says historian Henry Yu.[1] And yet, the quest for knowing still keeps Asian Americans' collective identity insecure and fragile. Asian America is in process that is ever changing in relation to the way American peoplehood is ever changing. The cultural identity of Asian Americans a as "a sense that [the physical location] is elsewhere" is indeed the driving force behind the second epistemological scaffold of the spirit of dissonance and dissent for the exploration of Asian Americans' second language. The absence of stability is what Asian Americans' second language and our diasporic existence are about. Asian America is always in process and a constantly shifting designation.[2] Postcolonial cultural theorist Stewart Hall's definition of cultural identity as "positioning" holds true for Asian Americans' diasporic identity. We do not necessarily see our identity as a mark of stability or ethnicity. "Cultural identity is not an essence but *positioning*. Hence, there is always a politics of identity, a politics of position, which has no absolute guarantee

1. Yu, *Thinking Orientals*, v.
2. Ibid., 13.

in an unproblematic, transcendental 'law of origin,'" says Hall.[3] Identity as positioning is shaped by the "historical reformulations of modern America, both as it has modified itself with regard to Asia and as Asians in America have variously affected its refiguration," says comparative literature scholar David Palumbo-Liu.[4] In other words, Asian Americans' identity cannot be objectified or essentialized. Our cultural identity as positioning is politicized, racialized, and often subversive in character against a prescribed notion of the American peoplehood. Asian American identity is intimately related to immigration law, racism, economic and social politics, and cultural practices of a wider society of America in which Asian America exits. "As conceptual entities with which (and against which) America measured itself, and *also* as active agents, Asians in America have historically participated in the constitution of what 'America' was and is at any given moment."[5] This symbiotic notion of our diasporic identity as it relates to the "refiguration" of America and its peoplehood provides a clue to the exploration into the emergence of Asian Americans' second language.

Claiming the particular position as a cloak of identity reveals the painful disjuncture between Asian Americans' longing for "knowledge, a secure place to be" and the realization that such knowledge and security are not likely attainable in the formulation of modern America. The disjuncture invites a rapport of Asian Americans with those other members of our society who share this precarious dilemma of being caught between the longing for security and reality of not being able to fulfill the longing. This dilemma, at the same time, helps Asian Americans critique the dominant ideology of a secure and stable identity that is tied with a particular location or ethnicity. Asian Americans' disjunctive and discordant experiences of the desire for a secure identity and the realization of the un-attainability of such security are at once externally imposed and internally situated. On the one hand, the instabilities are imposed by the racialized contradictory perceptions of Asian Americans in this society seen as both "a foreigner within" and "a model minority" at the same time, as we saw in the previous chapter. We are likely to be seen as a foreigner even if we are born in the U.S. or immigrated from Asia. "Where are you from?" is not a simple question of curiosity asked of an

3. Hall, "Cultural Identity and Diaspora," 226.
4. Palumbo-Liu, *Asian/American*, 1.
5. Yu, *Thinking Orientals*, 2.

Asian American. The question is fraught with the unspoken assumption that we are foreigners in this land thus outsiders to this society. "Considering the continuing exoticization of Asian Americans . . . it is unlikely that Orientals will ever been seen as white," says Yu.[6] This perception is part and parcel of America's redefinition of itself in the modern age as a nation faced toward the Pacific. On the other hand, we are likely to be treated as "model minority" immigrants who are exemplary to those other immigrants and minority populations who are disruptive in society even though a large number of Asian Americans live in an underprivileged sector of the American society. The emergence of the "model minority" thesis reflects a "sociological explanation of Asian American success and the failures of blacks in America, and reads this thesis in the context of both Civil Rights policies and the ascension of the Japanese economy," says Palumbo Liu.[7] This contradiction between the foreigners within and the model minority is also internally situated experiences for Asian Americans because of our own awareness of the "physical location of the unknown," namely the diasporic experiences of unsettledness. Within this disjuncture wells up the realization of Asian Americans being not fitting in the wider society, the realization that in turn leads to the emergence of the "spirit" of dissonance and dissent, or the impulse behind positioning of our identity that serves as a scaffold for the construction and emergence of our second language. If the racialized translocal existence of Asian Americans and our rupturally liminal experiences set the locus of the birth of our version of the second language, the dissonant and dissenting spirit of identity that emerges out of this place of diasporic disjuncture is the force that feeds the birth of our own language.

The sense of dissonance, not "fitting in," is common to racially and culturally disfranchised people in America. Native Americans, Hispanic Americans, Pacific Islanders, Arab Americans, and other racially, culturally, and sexually marginalized people have also shared a similar experience. Our "racial uniforms" and particular cultural orientations exacerbate our experiences of dissonance with the dominant culture.[8] The "veil" that W. E. B. Du Bois talks about in his *Souls of Black Folk*

6. Ibid.

7. Palumbo-Liu, *Asian/American*, 1.

8. The term "racial uniform" was first introduced by Robert Park of University of Chicago.

points to this dissonance for African Americans. "The key difference between the concept of the marginal man [sic] and double consciousness is... [that] rather than naming Marginal Man's cultural conflict between old and new worlds, Du Bois's concept explicitly connects double consciousness and political power: while the American black was part of a nation without power, they were also nationals without citizenship."[9] The veil is the particular act of political positioning for African Americans "to merge his double self into a better, a truer self... He simply wishes to make it possible for a man to be both a Negro and an American."[10] The collective identity of Asian Americans is also expressed in our racialized and politicized experiences. While whites enjoy ethnicity as voluntary and optional, Asian Americans continue to face perceptions and expectations from others to be culturally different because of our visible ethnic, racial, and cultural markers. Being perceived as forever being a foreigner or not being a "real" American, Asian Americans risk the marginalization and exclusion from America's ethnic and racial center in a distinct ways unlike some other people of color. We become "Orientals." This dissonant experience takes on the spirit of dissent that is subversive in character within the dominant cultural context of the U.S. Dissonance is, in other words, not simply the sense of unsettledness, "not fitting in" we experience in our lives. It is also expressed as a protest against the prescribed reading of the security of life is by the dominating racial and cultural groups. It is a dissenting spirit. In this chapter we will explore this spirit of dissonance and dissent.

THE FRAGILE NATURE OF THE ASIAN AMERICAN INTERPRETIVE PARADIGM

The spirit of dissonance and dissent appears in various spheres of our existence. This spirit points to the fragile nature of Asian American diasporic interpretive paradigm of life. The spirit, for example, constitutes the character of Asian American intellectual, cultural, and religious discourse that disrupts the assumption of what constitute an accepted canon. Because Asian American discourse on knowledge and faith is inextricably bound to the material contexts of racism, stereotyping and

---

9. Palumbo-Liu, *Asian/American*, 299.
10. Du Bois, *Souls of Black Folk*, 102.

social history, it resists a formal canonization. The discourse functions to critique academic abstraction and refuses to be subsumed under the familiar methods of intellectual, cultural, and religious studies. "This is why it is essential to acknowledge the constellation of relationships among colonialism, the plantation political economy, and the religious experiences of [Asian Americans,]" says Rudi Busto.[11] The spirit of dissonance and dissent exposes "all religious, ideological, or scholarly standpoints [that are] eventually [these standpoints are] re-inscribed in new, complex, and at times conflicting strategies," says Buddhist scholar Bernard Faure.[12] At the same time, the materially oriented spirit of dissonance and dissent brings us to a fuller understanding and appreciation for Asian American intellectual and religious experience as we will see later in this chapter.

This spirit is tempered by the history of exclusion, a paradoxical notion of expedient and sometimes self-serving acceptance of Asian Americans by a greater America, racial stereotyping, and myriad of other tragic experiences we have endured in history. If the irreducibility of race applies primarily to the African American experiences, in Asian American experiences of race are framed in terms of the establishment and nurturing of our own communities, including faith communities, that have been formed out of our diasporic existence in relation to the construction of America. Asian American communities, faith communities in particular, serve as the impetus for the emergence of this spirit of dissonance and dissent against the totalizing tendency of the wider society.[13] Literary narratives written by Asian Americans, for example, have attempted to invent images of Asian America that both delineate the boundaries Asian America and envision particular modes of crossing them into a wider America. This is to say that this spirit of dissonance and dissent is concomitant with our common religious impulses and serves as the primary driving force for the impermanent understanding of our place in the American peoplehood.

In the postcolonial discourse, the term "diaspora" refers mainly to the political and cultural situations arising from Western colonialism of the nineteenth and twentieth centuries. Diasporic moves are defined invariably as a displacement from the underprivileged former colonized

---

11. Busto, "Disorienting Subjects," 24.
12. Faure, *Chan Insights and Oversights*, 151.
13. Jeung, *Faithful Generations*, 5.

nations to the formerly colonialist west, particularly to its metropolitan centers.[14] "[D]iasporas . . . have found a home away from home in the very heartland of former colonialism."[15] However, this is only one picture of diaspora. Not all diaspora is necessarily exilic. Displacement is either forced upon us or voluntarily entered into. Displacement may be caused by the geopolitical and globalized economic conditions of a particular time. Asian diaspora today is more likely to be tied with the globalized process of economy, politics, and immigration than the traditional pattern of exile out of necessity or by coercion. The political clout of overseas communities of Asians has become a crucial source of foreign exchange for Asian economies. Moreover, the development of new Asian diasporic communities from New York to Tokyo is challenging national identity politics in unanticipated ways. Some Asian diasporic communities encompass several generations of immigration, others are "post-65" émigré, either way as a result of politicized forced displacement or as voluntary immigration. Furthermore, the existence of Asian Americans of the post-immigrant generations adds to the complexity of the term "diaspora" to describe Asian American communities. Many of these Asian Americans, particularly those who are born in the U.S., do not necessarily consider themselves as a diasporic person. Nevertheless, there is something disjunctive about their lives. The image of Asian Americans no matter where we were born, a "perpetual foreigner," certainly reinforces the disjunction. In other words, the lives of Asian Americans are translocal in character regardless of our generational differences.

No matter how diasporic communities are established, an assumption underlying diaspora discourse is that there is something inherently disjunctive, subversive and therefore simultaneously liberating and liminal about the disjunctive experiences and practices. This is so because the presence of people of color in the predominant North

---

14. Rajagopolan Radhakrishnan evokes "diasporic subjectivity" from the vantage point of his personal history as a professor of American literature from India who, "interpellated by the ideology of Western humanism," chose to go West where he switched to the teaching of theory and postcoloniality. Radhakrishnan, *Diasporic Mediations*, xvi.

15. Ibid., 174. In the introduction to *Displacement, Diaspora, and Geographies of Identities*, Smadar Lavie and Ted Swedenburg are likewise concerned with the diasporas that result from "massive migrations by racialized non-white subjects into the heart of Eurocenter" (Lavie and Swedenburg, "Introduction," 2).

Atlantic American landscape necessarily challenges the homogeneity of whiteness and "from heterogeneous ethnic enclaves, the minority strikes back, resisting the center's violent attempts to assimilate or destroy it."[16] Accordingly, diaspora offers "new frames of analysis that resist and transcend national boundaries through their creative articulations of practices that demonstrate possible modes of corroding the Eurocenter by actively Third-Worlding it."[17] This also applies to the sphere of religious life. Religious visionaries wrestle with the quandary of identities "between" ideas, cultures, religious systems, generations, nations, and even time frames. Whether we are speaking of individuals or whole communities of faith, "faith" for diasporic communities goes far beyond the traditionally transmitted religious practices of ritual, text, or sacrament of the established faith communities. Religious transformation in diasporic communities continue working through "between and among things": between and among traditions, between and among the institution and vernacular practices of domestic space, between and among the schematizations of academics and the "messiness" of everyday life, and between and among the relationship of humanity, the sacred, and the holy—between and among the "old countries" and diverse make-up of "America." In other words, diaspora as the interpretive paradigm of Asian America is quite unstable and fluid as we shall see in the next chapter under the theme of amphiboly.

This is not to say that there is a similarity of values and vision among diverse diasporic groups that exert similar kinds of subversive effects on the existing power structures. Characteristics such as deterritoriality, heterogeneity, hybridity, and multiplicity that are predicated on the translocal condition are often celebrated for their transgressive power and effect among various Asian American ethnic groups. But we also need to note that different groups entertain different power relations to the dominant group depending on a vast array of historical, political, economic and cultural factors.[18] Heterogeneity of translocal experiences straddles multiple spheres beyond the binary colonizer/

16. Lavie and Swendenburg, "Introduction," 10.

17. Ibid., 15.

18. A case in point is the conception of new ethnicities, which Stuart Hall articulates within the British-Caribbean context. Using examples of the works of black British filmmakers, Hall shows how a new Caribbean ethnicity grounded in "positional, conditional and conjectural" difference (447) may challenge the hegemonic conception of "Englishness." See Hall, "New Ethniticities," 441–49.

colonized divide. Managing the translocal and hybridized identities of Asian Americans is a highly complex balancing act involving negotiations of different kinds that are informed and influenced by the interests of a group, the newly-found home and the our ethnic differences.

And the cultural as well as religious transformations and innovations of Asian American work through the pregnant predicaments of our racialized translocality and ruptural liminality, "between and among things." The translocal, nomadic, and hybridized positional identities of Asian Americans create a counter-discourse that is not likely to depend on or at least admit to the dominant discourse for legitimization. These identities may deny the structures and texts of the traditional religious and theological discourses in favor of their own authentic experiences. In these identities there is room to move and breathe new life and interpretations into ancient stories both of the Abrahamic and Asian cosmologies away from the censor of the established north Atlantic religious and theological canons. The new interpretations take place primarily in the actual lived practices of faith communities and not necessarily in an academic setting. And in so doing so, Asian Americans pay homage to a world that—despite the corrosive powers of the modern and postmodern predicaments—has manage to survive and still can proclaim our own voices and experiences.

Another word of caution for the diaspora and translocal discourse is the use of a particular religious paradigm to interpret a translocal experience and practice. Scholars of religious and theological studies are especially susceptible to the danger of imposing a familiar paradigm in order to interpret a diasporic and translocal experience and practice out of one's deep investment in faith convictions. The exodus motif is a typical example of such a practice. "There is no Israel without the conquest of Canaan and the expulsion or inferior status of Canaanites – then as now," says Edward Said in his critique of Michael Walzer's work, *Exodus and Revolution*.[19] Walzer's claim is that the Exodus narrative has been understood and is about the observable consequences for radical politics. This is the danger of reading Exodus into history, says Said. Such a use of the Exodus as an interpretive paradigm is symptomatic of its apologetic character where "the movement from Egypt to Canaan is taken as a metaphor for a transforming politics."[20] That is to say that

19. Said, "Michael Walzer's *Exodus and Revolution*," 87.
20. Ibid., 93.

Walzer views the nature of the contemporary Israeli state by recasting the Exodus story as "the birth of a new policy, one that admits its members to a communal politics of participation in political and religious spheres."[21] Such a religious narrative may or may not serve as an appropriate interpretive framework of ethnic, racial, and national solidarities for certain diasporic and translocal groups. The Exodus is a historically particular paradigm that is not readily transferable to another context. What would happen if Egypt were the "promised land," an archetype of the Promised Land? By ignoring this question, there is a danger of downplaying the sense in which Egypt itself was a prototype, an earlier promised land, where the Israelites multiplied and prospered.

Said's critique of the Exodus paradigm even goes further. He critiques the bloodthirsty character of monotheistic politics, Yahweh's blood lust being carried over to the Christian God's blood lust and Allah's blood lust as well. Said's critique goes to the undesirability of monotheistic politics as such makes the "secular and decent politics" less likely. The question is how to separate the conquest of the land of Canaan, an essential part of the Exodus story, from "the attitudes of the murderous Puritans or of the founders of *apartheid*."[22] Though highly polemical in approach, Said rightly questions the moral quality of the Exodus story's political and ethical legacy. The critique of the unexamined Exodus paradigm is really to resist the temptation of being comfortably at home among one's people, supported by known powers and acceptable values, and protected against the outside world. This cautionary note of Said also speaks to Asian America in our faith articulations on our diasporic experiences. There are other frames of reference than the Exodus that serve as a more accurate and appropriate instrument for an analysis of Asian Americans' faith consciousness and practice. Stuart Hall coins the term "the positions of *enunciation*" to describe the practices of representation of emergent subject of Diaspora.[23] Rudy Busto talks about the defining characteristic of Chicano(a)/Latino(a) and Filipino American religions as that of "predicament."[24] Lisa Lowe, commenting on the character of Asian American literature, talks about "the shifting position of dialectical criticism, [that] can neither immerse itself in the object in

---

21. Ibid., 87.
22. Ibid.
23. Hall, "Cultural Identity and Diaspora," 392.
24. Busto, "The Predicament of Neplanta," 238.

the manner of idealizing, redemptive criticism nor take a stand entirely outside culture to criticize the totality as reified."²⁵ Lowe argues for the "contradictions that produce these particulars [that] demand a different notion of the aesthetics of Asian immigrant work..."²⁶ Diasporic Asian Americans display at least four representative components in its frame of reference: (1) the sense of dislocation in one's own home, (2) an act of imagining past this "predicament" in search of ways to avoid despair, and (3) a heightened sensitivity toward the pathos not only one's own experiences but also of neighbors and neighboring communities who are also diasporic, and (4) possibly, the cadences of new social possibility based on a new way of relating with others.

For Asian Americans, the construction of our collective identity, a shared notion of allegiance, solidarity, and affiliation, as it is permeated by racialized creation of our own communal space, is likely to be associated with particular kind of religious impulse, or spirit, that is the spirit of dissonance and dissent. This spirit serves as the basic interpretive paradigm of our diasporic life. Religious consciousness is the way of thinking characteristic of collective existence. "[T]here is plausibility to the notion that racialized and diasporic identities and histories and narratives operate along lines similar to civil religion," notes David Kyuman Kim.²⁷ This "civil religion" arises out of our experiences of incongruity between our desire for acceptance and the reality of not fitting in to the dominant culture. Here the operative frames of analysis is racialized identities, trnaslocal and nomadic hybridity, and fluidity of Asian American identities that trigger religious impulses through the traditioning process of a "larger memory" making, a shared history and values that are being internalized and ritualized by Asian Americans.

DISLOCATION AT HOME & THE REFUSAL TO DISPEAR

However an overarching paradigm existing within the established religious traditions, may it be within the Abrahamic faith traditions or in Asian DNAs of our non-theistic cosmological and religious traditions, does not adequately serve as an accurate instrument to understand

---

25. Lowe, *Immigrant Acts*, 32.
26. Ibid.
27. Kim, "Enchanting Diasporas," 331.

Asian American religious consciousness. An uncritical use of an existing religious narrative in history does injustice to an accurate reading of what goes on in Asian American religious scene. The spirit of dissonance and dissent as a significant interpretive paradigm is gradually emerging as an appropriate frame of analysis that is being shaped in the process of collective cultural identity making among Asian Americans. The spirit is "contrapuntal" as Edward Said describes it, occurring "against the memory of these things in another environment."[28] It is also a plurality of vision that gives rise to an awareness of simultaneous dimensions of life.

> *I look at my grandfather*
> *First generation*
> *Proud old issei man*
> *His English is bad*
> *Movements*
> *Very slow and sure*
> *His mind*
> *Full of the world*
> *He looks at me*
> *Third generation*
> *Proud young sansei*
> *His Japanese is bad*
> *He is so quick*
> *Too sure of himself*
> *So much to learn*
> *In him*
> *I can see my heritage*
> *My soul*
> *In me*
> *He can see his youth*
> *His life.*[29]

A shared experiences of pathos, "In him I can see my heritage, my soul. In me, he can see his youth, his life" is likely to shape a collective sense of cultural and religious consciousness, the plurality of vision that kindles the religious impulse of translocal Asian Americans. This pathos is, in the words of Homi Bhabha, " a bridge, where 'presencing' begins because it captures something of the estranging sense of dislocation and the relocation of the home and the world—the absence of secure home—

---

28. Said, *Reflections on Exile and Other Essays*, 186.
29. Nishikawa, "Grandfather," 54.

that is the condition of extra-territorial and cross-cultural initiations."[30] Dislocation, relocation of the home, and one's refusal to despair in the condition of predicament are interrelated one with another. Dislocation, along with the sense of being racially other, reminds Asian Americans that certitude is not really attainable, that privileges are fleeting commodities, and at the same time, dominant powers are increasingly ineffective, existing institutions seem less and less to deliver what is intended and long counted upon. Even the relocation of the home does not seem to create a new social possibility. We are still being "perpetual foreigners" at home. Home is not really home. "At-homeness" is an unattainable goal. Sadness, rage, and loss are operative feelings. To make the situation even worse, this society seems to lack ways of thinking and ways of speaking that can give us remedial access to this predicament. How does one avoid despair so as not to be defeated in life? *In him I can see my heritage. My soul. In me He can see his youth His life.* Communities and familial relationships, particularly religious communities, are formed to mitigate the nomadic loneliness, the raging racism, and despair. Some refuse to accept the impossibility of change and strive toward social and racial justice even in the midst of what seems an impossiblity. This is Asian Americans' experience of life in diaspora. This is the spirit of dissent that is coupled with the spirit of dissonance.

J. Craig Fong, a gay Asian American, articulates such a spirit in his reflective essay "Becoming an ancestor."[31]

> Being Asian and being queer are a different set of interests and balances. I'm not saying that it's easier or harder. But it's different. How you deal with those differences is something you look to other Asians to help you with because white folks don't understand.

What is different for Fong is the Confucian and Buddhist roots of the Asian cultures that impinges upon the issues of sexuality.

> [Y]ou are nothing until you become an ancestor. If I don't make my father an ancestor—what that means is giving him a grandson. So that when my father dies, my son will grow up remembering and revering his grandfather ... And you don't become an ancestor until you have people alive today worshipping you when you are dead. So the idea, even for me, a fourth generation Chinese

---

30 Bhabha, *The Location of Culture*, 9.
31 Fong, 357–58.

American, that I will never be an ancestor. Why? Because I don't have kids. Who will burn incense on my grave?

Fong recalls a Holocaust poster he once saw hanging on the office wall of a friend that depicts signs commemorating persons who died of AIDS with a candle surrounded by barbed wire. The inscription reads: "Who Will Say Kaddish For Me?"

> That's exactly it. Who is going to say Kaddish for me? Who is going to burn incense at my grave? It's not about the future. It's about the past. It's about maintaining a link to the people who came before you. When we try to explain that to the mainstream gay and lesbian community, they don't get it. And that is the Asian equivalent of 'Who Will Say Kaddish For Me?. . . .
>
> You become brave. You remind yourself that it is not so much whether or not your family burns incense at your grave. You condition yourself to remember that the honor and memory to who you are lives on in those who continue after you. . .
>
> And those people who remember your contribution are those who will symbolically burn incense at your grave. And those are the people you need to cultivate now. Because most of us, as Asian gay men and lesbians, will not have children.[32]

A hybridized notion of the sacred (Confucian & Buddhist roots of Asian cosmology coupled with the Jewish practice of Kaddish) is the context in which the discovery of the "being an ancestor" is made for Fong:

> I would say what is probably the best lesson to be taken away from this, is that finding your identity is an exercise in great courage. It is particularly so for marginalized people, for minorities, for people doubly marginalized.[33]

Being Asian American and being gay situate Fong and other gay Asian Americans in a peculiar social setting that is a "physical location of the unknown, a sense that it is elsewhere." "If you're talking about who is the gay community marginalizes Asian Pacific Islanders, I would say gay and lesbian mainstream white people do."[34] Added to the fact that Asian American and Pacific Islanders population is relatively small, the gay and lesbian community is particularly a minority in representation. ". . . because the mainstream white community, especially in the gay and

32. Ibid.
33. Ibid.
34. Ibid.

lesbian community, have certain stereotypes about what Asian Pacific Islanders are. And those stereotypes work distinctly against us."[35] Then, there is also a prejudice against gays and lesbians that exist within Asian American communities. Caught between these two forces,

> Being Asian and being queer are a different set of interests and balances. I'm not saying that it's easier or harder. But it's different. How you deal with those differences is something you look to other Asians to help you with because white folks don't understand.[36]

The spirit of dissonance and dissent as the absence of home is expressed by Fong and other Asian American gays and lesbians as "becoming brave," and conditioning oneself "to remember that the honor and memory to who you are lives on in those who continue after you." The struggle for identity as an Asian American gay or lesbian is this: "However you want to slice that, it's an exercise in courage of all of us to find, nurture, cultivate and ultimately adopt the identities and beliefs that make us up as human beings." The spirit of dissent arises out of this exercise in courage.

Activist Yuri Kochiyama's life also exemplifies such a diasporic experience of Asian Americans and the underlying spirit of life. At age 78 and as a recent visiting scholar with UCLA's Asian American Studies Center and a Nobel Peace Prize nominee of 2005, Yuri Kochiyama began to write her memoir for her family. *Passing It On: A Memoir* is the account of this extraordinary Asian American woman who spoke out and fought shoulder-to-shoulder with African Americans, Native Americans, Latinos, Asian Americans, and whites for social justice, civil rights, and prisoner and women's rights in the United States and internationally for more than half a century.[37] Kochiyama's life reflects the pain of dislocation, her willingness to imagine past despair, her desire to connect with those who are in a similar circumstance, and then to strive toward social justice. The daughter of Japanese immigrants, Kochiyama was born in San Pedro, California in 1921. The FBI arrested her father during World War II and labeled him a "prisoner of war." After interrogating him for several weeks and finding no cause for his arrest, they

---

35. Ibid.
36. Ibid.
37. Kochiyama, *Passing It On*.

released him. Seiichi Nakahara died several days after his arrest. "As I reflect back on that traumatic event, I see the parallel between the way African Americans were treated in the segregated South and the way Japanese Americans were evacuated and relocated en masse to remote internment camps, across the U.S.," Kochiyama wrote.[38] "In each instance, there was senseless degradation, brutality, and hatred wrought by fear and ignorance caused by racism."[39]

In 1942 Kochiyama and her family were forcibly removed from their homes and imprisoned in internment camp in Jerome, Arkansas. Kochiyama notes that seventy percent of those removed were American citizens and the remaining thirty percent were Japanese immigrants who had been denied the possibility of citizenship. In 1946 she married Bill Kochiyama, a World War II veteran she had met at the camp. The couple settled in New York City, Bill's hometown, and had six children. In 1960 the Kochiyamas moved to a new low-income housing project in Harlem. Yuri and Bill Kochiyama became active in the Harlem Parents Committee, which created its own school to protest the quality of public schools in Harlem. The Kochiyama family supported numerous other political and social causes in Harlem through protests, demonstrations and other organizing efforts. They picketed schools in Harlem to demand a better education. They hosted a talk by the Freedom Riders, an interracial group of activists from throughout the United States who boarded buses headed for the South in order to protest the practice of segregated public transportation. On their way to visit relatives back in California, Kochiyamas took their children to visit the Baptist church in Birmingham, Alabama where four girls were killed in a bombing. "I believe our children who grew up in Harlem had one advantage: they were in the circumference of the civil rights movement," Yuri Kochiyama wrote. "Harlem was a university without walls."[40]

In 1965 two of Kochiyamas' oldest children, Billy and Audee, went to Mississippi to register African Americans to vote. The family also took part in numerous marches to commemorate the atomic bombings of Hiroshima and Nagasaki and protested against the Vietnam War. In 1971 one of the couple's children, Eddie, visited China with the Progressive Student Delegation, which was only the second American group to be

38. Ibid., 7.
39. Ibid.
40. Ibid., 65.

allowed to visit China after the country's Cultural Revolution. In 1977 Yuri Kochiyama took part in the take-over of the Statue of Liberty by Puerto Rican independence activists who were demanding the release of activist Andre Cordero, who was dying of cancer.

Yuri also talked about her family's association with Malcolm X. In 1964 the Kochiyama family was hosting three writers of the Hiroshima/Nagasaki World Peace Study Mission and the writers wanted to meet Malcolm X. On the day of the meeting of the writers, Malcolm X showed up, spoke with the journalists, and took pictures with people who had gathered at the Kochiyamas' home. Malcolm X developed a friendship with the family and sent them eleven postcards from his travels abroad. On Feb. 21, 1965, Yuri was there when Malcolm X gave a speech at the Audubon Ballroom. "I was in the audience when Malcolm X was assassinated and immediately ran on stage as soon as he fell to the floor," Kochiyama wrote. "Cradling his head in my hands, I was shocked."[41] Yuri also recalls the tragic deaths of her two children and her son-in-law, Alkamal. She supported political prisoners by writing letters to various prisoners and visiting them. She also visited Cuba and Peru, and has been involved in the Asian American Movement. Yuri Kochiyama is an embodiment of Asian American diasporic life and the spirit of dissonance and dissent: dislocation, being not at home in one's home, refusal to acquiesce to despair, cross-racial community building in her heightened sense of pathos toward those who are also displaced, and strife toward social and racial justice. In her life the spirit of dissonance and dissent arises as the power of new social possibility.

Asian Americans comprise a complicated interplay and collision of different identities. We do not fit in a hierarchy of identities led by ethnic-based narratives. Our subjectivity claims are non-unitary unlike the coherent identity images that find expression in much talk and writing about American racial and ethnic groups. What can be said about us is the high value we place on brevity and courage that are needed for our self-representation and subjectivity claims. "[I]t's an exercise in courage of all of us to find, nurture, cultivate and ultimately adopt the identities and beliefs that make us up as human beings."[42] This is the spirit and impulse that undergirds our lives based on our shared experiences and histories as Asian Americans.

41. Ibid., 72.
42. Ibid., 173.

"TRANSCENDENTAL UNHOMEDNESS" AND COMMUNITY BUILDING[43]

Religious symbols serve as an intensification of these shared experiences and histories of Asian Americans. These symbols are ritualized for their transmission within the communities and are then transmitted into subsequent generations thereby aiding our reflective practices of life meanings. These religious symbols are powerful expressions of Asian Americans' tradition-building, *actus tradendi*. Tradition-construction indeed "represent[s] the becoming and transformation of dispersed and racialized peoples through a symbolization that marks a renewed engagement and participation within the cultural and political realities of late modernity for Asian Americans," according to Bhabha.[44] To be sure, Asian Americans experiences and our need to "reclaim history" are often diffuse, shifting, and sometimes contradictory. Thus, the diasporic experiences with their corresponding values, morality, and worldviews that arise out of them, along with community and institution building in a racialized society, serve as a powerful agent for the emergence of a distinct communal coherence and tradition-making but in a "messy" fashion. Together, however, they represent the paradigmatic lens through which our diasporic existence is interpreted. But as such, the lens is tentative, temporal, and fragile serving as an interpretive instrument for the time being if it is to be true to our transitory diasporic and translocal experiences. Its lasting significance is yet to be determined.

> The Asian American identity as we now know it may not last another generation. Which makes doubters like me grow more doubtful—and more hopeful. There was something about the creation of this race, after all, that embodied the spirit of the times: compensatory, reactive, consumed with what Charles Taylor calls 'the politics of recognition.' There is something new about the mutation of the race that reflects a change in that spirit. . . . From the perspective of my children and their children, from the perspective, that is, of those who will be the synthesis, it may seem that 'Asian American' was but a cocoon: something useful, something to outgrow. And in this way, the future of the race may reflect the future of race itself. A future beyond recognition.[45]

---

43. The term "transcendental homelessness" was originally used by Lukacs in *Theory of Novel* and adopted by Said in *Reflections on Exile*, 181.

44. Bhabha, *The Location of Culture*, 332.

45. *The Accidental Asian: Notes of a Native Speaker*, 83.

A diasporic life is an alternative to the institutions that dominate modern life. It is "strangely compelling to think about but terrible to experience," says Edward Said.[46] It is terrible to experience because we really do not have home to go back to and, at the same time, we are not totally at home in the place we choose to live. It is "strangely compelling to think about" because it accords a person a particular angle of vision to see reality in impermanence, liminality, and dislocation. And yet, the diasporic life also offers a glimpse of freedom, intimacy, and possible originality of vision as noted in the previous illustrations.

How do we frame the understanding of diasporic life as a constitutive force of our collective cultural identity, of an ambiguous and tenuous attachment to each other as Asian Americans? The mediating factor is a capacity of translocal and diasporic person to viewing the world through what W. E. B. Du Bois calls a "double consciousness" that makes possible originality of vision. It is akin to Wallace Stevens' notion of "'a mind of winter' in which the pathos of summer and autumn as much as the potential of spring are nearby but unobtainable."[47] This realization results from a translocal person to long to be rooted in some secure place, "the most important and least recognized need of the human soul," as Simone Weil, noted.[48] And yet, remedies we seek for overcoming a quest for security are often just as dangerous and stifling as they are supposed to quench our thirst for being rooted, for these remedies not only tame one's sensibility to the vicissitude of life but, more importantly, alters one's life perspective.

> To be unhomed is not to be homeless, nor can the "unhomely" be easily accommodated in that familiar division of social life into private and public spheres. The unhomely moment creeps up on you stealthily as your own shadow and suddenly you find yourself with Henry James's Isabel Archer, in *The Portrait of a Lady*, taking the measure of your dwelling in a state of "incredulous terror."[49]

This is the predicament of Asian American diaspora that we share as our cultural marks creating a rapport beyond a politically motivated confederate alliance of ethnic and national differences. Moreover, "Asians

46. Said, *Reflections on Exile and Other Essays*, 173.
47. Said, quoting Wallace Stevens in *Reflections on Exile and Other Essays*, 186.
48. Ibid., 183.
49. Bhabha, *The Location of Culture*, 9.

have been admitted into the U.S. nation in terms of national economic imperatives, while the state has estranged Asian immigrants through racialization and bars to citizenship, thus distancing Asian Americans, even as citizens, from the terrain of national culture."[50] Due to this ironic paradoxical status, Asian Americans come together because there is an awareness that we together in choosing not between two opposite poles of racial and ethnic identities, not between the pure and the despoiled, but that our identity has to do with its impermanence, "a state of 'incredulous terror.'" It also has to do with a choice we have to make about what degree of "unhomely," in-betweeness, which of the innumerable possible combinations, what expression of hybridity we will bring into being. This is the texture of the spirit of dissonance and dissent. Attorney Angela E. Oh expresses this texture as "openness." "What has been the greatest gift in my life is openness. In this, I have found both pleasure and pain, inspiration and disappointment, laughter and tears. In short, I have found a way to grow. I recognize the gift of being blessed."[51]

This realization of "transcendental unhomedness" constitutes the major driving force for religious impulse and reflections for Asian Americans.[52] Located particularly in a society where values appear to be clear, identities unitary, stable and unquestioned most of the time, disinherited people seek to construct a new world that somewhat resembles an old one left behind. And yet the person is in a Catch 22 situation. S/he finds oneself of being in "distance from the terrain of national culture" and, at the same time, desires to speak of the religious and spiritual condition and consciousness of "unhomedness" of Asian American experience. Some seek to overcome this paradox by identifying themselves with and affiliating with the mainstream parties, mass institutions that dominate modern life, whereby diminishing critical perspective, of intellectual reserve, of moral courage. Others, sensing an urgent need to reconstitute a restored community, resort to a jealous and resentful isolation by creating an exclusive community of their own. Yet even there those who romanticize a solitude experienced outside of the dominant group risk trivialize the radical nature of the very solitude, the habit of dissonance. The question is this: What would it mean to consider collective identity formation in light of diaspora as religious and spiritual

50. Lowe, *Immigrant Acts*, 176.
51. Oh, *Open: One Woman's Journey*, 5.
52. Lukacs, *Theory of the Novel*.

enterprise that points to the fullness of life? This is the question regarding the veracity of faith communities for Asian Americans.

"When your [Chinese] father died, you realize this: it is the liquid of memory, not the cup we drink it from, that gives our lives content and reveals our humanity," remarks Eric Liu as he reflects on the death of his father.[53] Diasporic existence is a representation of a collective experience that symbolizes the spirit of Asian Americans. The memory of the past in the person of those who enter North America before our times serves as "the liquid of memory" that fuses with our experiences of the present to form the contour and content of who we are, our identities both as a person and as a community. But the memory of the past is fraught with the pain of displacement as it is juxtaposed with the experiences of interstice and vicissitudious existence of the present. It is, furthermore, incongruous with the value orientation prevalent in the larger society. This incongruity serves as a vehicle of religious consciousness.[54] It is a "different mirror," "the indeterminate temporality of the in-between," (Said) through which to view life.[55] In other words, the spirit of a fundamentally dissonant state of being, that homecoming is out of the question even in the newly found home, is no less than the sacred spirit in so far as it enables the creation and maintenance of collective existence. It functions as "totems that have an authority and power over the kinds of moral, political, and existential commitments and actions that Asian Americans will have."[56] The acknowledgement of such "unhomedness" is the glue, though temporal and fragile glue at that, that holds a group of people together. Our collective identity is a synthesis that can recombine, re-synthesize fluid ethnic and other social borders affected by the sentiments of affinity and estrangement.

However, a word of caution is in order. Rudy Busto points out that "Asian American and Pacific Islander religions refuse to be subsumed under the dominant methods and approaches of either Religious or Asian American studies as they have developed."[57] Unlike African American identity, Asian American cultural identities do not yet have a cultural idiom that arose from centuries of thinking themselves as a race.

53. Liu, *The Accidental Asian*, 31.
54. Smith, *Map Is Not Territory*, 301.
55. Takaki, *A Larger Memory*.
56. Kim, "Enchanting Diasporas," 334.
57. Busto, "Disorienting Subjects," 24.

Unlike Jewish identity, Asian Americans are yet to build a unifying spiritual and historical legacy that can be definable. Our collective identity is quite fleeting and has no guarantee of permanence. It is "something useful, something to outgrow," as Eric Liu comments. Vicissitudinous rapport that is emerging as the cultural foundation of our group identity amidst an incoherent appearance of "heterogeneity, hybridity, and multiplicity" is itself very tenuous. What will become of this rapport in the future is yet to be told just as the future of Asian American cultural identities is uncertain. If a cultural identity is as Stuart Hall claims is not "an essence but a positioning," we need to remind ourselves that Asian Americans' creation of a historical legacy is not only spiritual but also political. Here lies the complexity of the issue. "Disorienting subjects" is the term Rudy Busto uses to describe the insurgent character of Asian American religious experiences and orientations. The "disorienting" paradigm grows out of the nexus of the actual communal faith practices in conjunction with Asian American studies and religious studies. The study of Asian American religious traditions cannot survive without all of them. Just as the study and content of Asian American literature disrupts the assumptions of what constitutes a literary canon, and by its very existence resists appropriation by traditional academic disciplines, Asian Americans' "disorienting" paradigm is inextricably bound to its material contexts of labor, racism, stereotyping and social history. It is disorienting because it resists the formal abstraction of aestheticization and canonization. Quoting Buddhist scholar Bernard Faure, Busto observes that attending too rigorously to disciplinary paradigms and methods is limiting, and that eventually, "all religious, ideological, or scholarly standpoints are eventually re-inscribed in new, complex, and at times conflicting strategies."[58] "Ultimately, revealing is always hiding; any insight generates its own blindness; any deconstruction is always already a reconstruction."[59]

At least this can be said: The sense of diasporic vicissitude, that is, the spirit of dissonance and dissent, challenges the prevailing sociotaxonomic order as it infiltrates the interstices of a given social structure and values by revealing the inadequacies, contradictions and arbitrary nature of such structure and values. For those who are moved by the spirit of dissonance and dissent, they know that the emperor indeed

58. Ibid.
59. Ibid.

does not have a cloth. The sense of translocal vicissitude creates a realm of competing discourse, a field of communal relations, a collective identity that is alternative to the prevailing dominant institutions. This is akin to what Homi Bhabha claims; "focusing on those interstitial moments or processes that are produced in the articulation of 'differences.' . . . How are subjects formed 'in-between' or in excess of, the sum of the 'parts' of difference (usually intoned as race/class/gender/etc.)?"[60] Bhabha's emphasis of the role of historical agency in this in-between person accurately describes the collective identity formation of Asian Americans. How is it different from a more stable cultural identity besides its function of de-legitimizing the existing socio-taxonomic order? Can it constructively participate in the creation of a new order that is an alternative to a deeply engrained instinct for classification?

Lisa Lowe argues that understanding Asian immigration to the United States is fundamental to understanding the racialized economic and political foundations of the nation. As stated earlier, the spirit of dissonance and dissent arises out of the contradictions whereby Asians have been included in the workplaces amid markets of the U.S. nation-state, yet, through exclusion laws and bars from citizenship, have been distanced from the terrain of national culture. Understanding these contradictions lays the clues for the contributions of Asian diaspora before a larger society in the future.

> Historically, the U.S. state has constructed different national "emergencies" around "the immigrant," which have, over time, generated emergent political formations. Our critical task now is to make the present *emergency* an active state of *emergence* in ways that respond to the contemporary conditions of global restructuring—conditions that exploit Asian workers both in Asia *and* in the deindustrialized United States, that bring new waves of immigrants from Asia and Latin America where precisely the United States has been a colonial or neocolonial power, and that intensify exploitation and worklessness in the United States in ways that exacerbate interracial urban conflicts. Our work begins with an engagement with the past, out of which we imagine, create, and dare to secure a future.[61]

---

60 Bhabha, "Frontlines," 269.
61. Lowe, *Immigrant Acts*, 176.

"In the sharing of our varied stories, we create our community of a larger memory," says Ronald Takaki.[62] Given the distance from the American national culture that Asian Americans experience, does this comment by Takaki also apply to a wider societal scene beyond Asian American diaspora? What sort of future does Asian American culture have as an alternative site that produces cultural forms materially and aesthetically in contradiction with the institutions of citizenship and national identity? "What happens here, of course, is not *inherently* blessed. It is only the future," says Eric Liu[63] Perhaps so. We shall next look at the role of ritualization of the spirit of dissonance to respond to the role of American Asians' collective identity for a wider society and its future.

RITUALIZATION OF RELIGIOUS IMPULSES: PARTICIPATION IN THE EMERGENCE OF "A LARGER MEMORY"

The spirit of dissonance and dissent as the cohering religious energy of Asian American cultural consciousness seeks to find its stability in its ritualization within their institutions of which faith communities are integral part. Dissonance or what Said calls "contrapuntal" reading of life is not a readily appreciated consciousness in the society. It is often misunderstood and dismissed as irrelevant and absurd. Yet that which does not tidily fit into the accepted consciousness and values is still there and demands attention. Rituals function as means of reclaiming what is rejected by a larger society and is ploughed back for a renewal of life. An act of ritualizing is making of new forms through which the valued pattern and its panoply of associations of certain expressive behavior can flow. The religious impulse of Asian Americans is revealed in the ritual practices that are an attempt to force our experiences into the realm of sacrality.

At the same time that ritual creates order it also recognizes the potency of disorder. Creative formlessness is as much symbol of beginning and growth as it is of decay. Reflecting on the Tule Lake Pilgrimage, a visit to the once infamous detention camp of Japanese and Japanese Americans during World War II, theologian Joanne Doi notes:

---

62 Takaki, *A Larger Memory*, 353.

63. Liu, *Accidental Asian*, 202.

> The Tule Lake Pilgrimage is a ritual process of inhabiting the interstices in a collective way that reveal to ourselves and others the past contradictions and arbitrariness of a societal structure that saw us as dangerous anomalies and that in large part were the cause of the imprisonment of persons of Japanese ancestry based on their ancestry.[64]

A ritual object or action becomes sacred by having attention focused on it in a highly marked way. This is Jonathan Smith's notion that ritual is a mode of paying attention, a process for making interest.[65] The tenuous and fluid state of the collective cultural identity of Asian Americans yeans for a ritual of sacralization. The cultural identity is not a formless and nebulous entity. It is narrative specific. Its transmission occurs through memorialization and ritualized communal act of sharing. "Sacrality is above all, a category of emplacement."[66] Sacred place is indeed "storied place."[67] Sociologist Russell Jeung quotes a pastor of a Protestant commenting on the popularity of ethnic programs over traditional, Western Christian festivities.

> Last year, we did Halloween, Thanksgiving, Christmas and we were having like 40, 50 kids. When we did Mochizuki [rice pounding into cakes], we had 120 kids. So what does that tell me? Should we try to do this ethnic stuff or should we do this plain wrapper Christian stuff? We did 40, 50, 60 when we did Christian staff and we had a bigger number with ethnic stuff, so . . .[68]

Jeung comments that "Not only does ethnic culture affect church programming and worship style, but it also becomes the basis of church community and solidarity."[69] The religious impulse underlying the dissonant and precarious collective identity is ritualized for the recognition of its sacrality. The ritualized process of sacralization is, at the same time,

---

64. Doi, *Tule Lake Pilgrimage*, 28.

65. Smith, *To Take Place: Toward Theory in Ritual*. Smith values the exploration of the dimensions of incongruity in attempting to understand the complexity of such a construction. The perception of incongruity gives rise to thought as Ricoeur maintains and incongruity can serve as a vehicle of religious experience.

66. Ibid., 103.

67. Lane, *Landscapes of the Sacred*.

68. Jeung, "New Asian American Churches," 227.

69. Ibid., 228.

a "messy" process, no logical or straight line, but is filled with contradictions and incongruity.[70]

The question of identity is also a question of participation in ways of being in the world that are meaningful for communities as well as individuals and therefore calls for the transformation of moral visions.[71] "[T]hrough the transforming of moral visions—in the utopias and dystopias of diaspora and race—Asian Americans are striving to route their lives from the woundedness, absurdity, and despair of ambiguous alterity toward a sense of themselves that is spiritually and religiously meaningful and culturally profound."[72] Ritual is a powerful force for such a function. Ritual is a vital component in processes of social change.[73] It is a particular mode of discourse that effectively evokes sentiments of affinity or estrangement, actively creating, de-legitimizing certain previous practices, or reconstructing society. Ritual can be employed to encode and replicate the established structures and/or effective instruments of struggle in implementing change. Ritual can be employed to encode and replicate the established structures and/or effective instruments of struggle in implementing change. "The web of meaning," as Wittgenstein calls it, cannot locate itself all by itself, cannot answer to itself. It calls for something other than itself, something not linguistic, something outside, something before, alongside, or yet-to-be, which can summon language to be language, can communicate that it makes sense to explore without yet knowing what is latent. In this sense, ritualization of the spirit of dissonance for Asian diaspora in North America is subversive.

> Today we give birth to Korean Woman Jesus. And we will use a Korean traditional playground dramatic style throughout the worship service. What we are doing is just like Jesus who did not follow the law of the Sabbath.
>
> We, Women Church . . . practice a type of worship in which everybody can participate in the preaching and blessing together, and where people sit in a circle. We try to relate to our reality, and our situations of today, and listen to the voices of the least in our society.

---

70. Smith, *Map is Not Territory*, 301
71. Kim, "Enchanting Diasporas," 337.
72. Ibid.
73. Turner, "Body, Brain, and Culture," 21–25.

> Our practice is rooted in Jesus' declaration of a Sabbath which exists for people. We are working to establish a church which truly follows Jesus. We are women who have been oppressed for 5000 years, so we stand on the side of the oppressed. We are women who have been and are forced to serve within the hierarchical structure of churches, and so we will work to overcome those hierarchies. We are the women who can become pregnant and bear life, so we will continue to hold life precious. In it under these convictions that we establish the mission of Women Church today.[74]

To be aware of the otherness beyond the frontier, is necessary if an eventual intellectual cynicism is to be avoided. Such awareness is characteristics of the spirit of dissonance and dissent. Like Wittgenstein, the ground of all meaning is an ungrounded way of acting. Praxis and meaning are not separate for ritualization of the spirit of dissonance and dissent. Ritual for Asian Americans therefore carries an authoritative mode of symbolic discourse.[75] Ritualization is also liminal in character. In the novel, *Picture Bride,* novelist Yoshiko Uchida describes a predicament that a character in the novel, Kiku, experiences about her religious orientations and affiliations:

> Kiku confessed that she rarely went to church on Sundays because she could not sit through Reverend Okada's sermons. She had a small Buddhist shine in her living room, however, and occasionally lit incense there to pray for her ancestors. 'I guess I'm part-Buddhist, part-Christian and part nothing at all,' she laughed.[76]

It is a liminal space that Kiku finds herself in, a space that is both unsettling and intriguing. Recognizing interstitial, liminal, or vicissitudious entities, the sprint of dissonance and dissent goes unrecognized and defies the rules of a conventional classification, the existence of which such classification is incapable of acknowledging. Yet, the spirit of dissonance and dissent can de-legitimate the order as it lives in the interstices of the existing social system on the one hand and lived experiences on the other, revealing the inadequacies, contradictions, and arbitrary nature of the dominant structure.

74. Chang, Kim, and Chung, "Korean Woman Jesus," 45.
75. Lincoln, *Discourse and the Construction of Society,* 170–74.
76. Uchida, *Picture Bride,* 13.

"It is indeed a testimony to the enduring human spirit that, in spite of relentless marginalization, there have been Asian Americans who exercise their liminal creativity to struggle for justice and a space we call home," says theologian Sang Hyung Lee.[77] Liminality is characterized by a de-structuring in relation to what Turner calls "social structure" which is the sum total of rules, norms, and status-makers that society keeps in place to define and govern its institutions and to control the processes of material production. Ritualized liminality employs structures of its own; but these are different from the structures of society, and they are often utilized to emphasize equality, anonymity, and intimacy compared with status-marked intelligence of the social order. When people engage in ritual activity, they separate themselves, partially if not totally, from the roles and statuses they have in the workaday world. There is a threshold in time or space or both, and certainly a demarcation of behavior, over which people pass when entering into ritual. The day-to-day world, with its social structure, is temporarily suspended.

Maxine Hong Kingston in *The Woman Warrior*, describes Maxine, a Chinese American woman struggling to learn English, who is alienated alike from the Chinese world of her parents and the world of white Americans. In her reinterpretation of the legend of Ts'ai Yen, a poet amid barbarians, Maxine reconnects with her ancestral culture even in her conflicted life. Ts'ai Yen, captured by the nomadic barbarians place primitive pipes to their arrows, which make a terrible whistle in flight. Ts'ai Yen has thought that this noise is her captors' only music, until she hears, "music tremble and rise like desert wind."

> She hid in her tent but could not sleep through the sound. Then, out of Ts'ai Yen's tent, which was apart from the others, the barbarians heard a woman's voice singing, as if to her babies, a song so high and clear, it matched the flutes. Ts'ai Yen sang about China and her family there. Her words seemed to be Chinese, but the barbarians understood their sadness and anger.... She brought her songs back from the savage lands, and one of the three that has been passed down to us is 'Eighteen Stanzas for a Barbarian Reed Pipe,' a song that Chinese sing to their own instruments. It translated well.[78]

---

77. Lee, "Pilgrimage and Home in the Wilderness of Marginality," 219.
78. Kingston, *The Woman Worrier*, 243.

Caught in a cross-cultural web of Chinese and American ways of life, Maxine describes sadness, anger, and fear "so high and clear." Even "the barbarians understood [her] sadness and anger." She reconnects with her ancestral heritage. In her struggle across two distinct cultures and worldviews, Maxine seeks to emulate the poet who sings to foreign music. Her Chinese song and music symbolizing the heritage and her imaginations "translated well" even in the place of dislocation.

Russell Jeung points out that ". . . symbols are not fixed, but are subject to infusions of new meaning and reinterpretation. Symbolic racial identities may also be recast when certain symbols become less salient and new ones emerge within a group."[79] Because ritual is essentially imaginative, it does not constitute a realm entirely independent of social structure. The terms of its imagination takes their initial cues from mundane life, and the time of ritual is but a limited time. When it is over, the duties pertaining to the social structure must resume. Hence ritual activity, existing as if outside the structures of society, existing in a subjunctive mode of imagination and pretend, is liminal.

Reflecting on the role of a Chinese Buddhist temple in southern California, Dharma Light Temple, Sociologist Carolyn Chen comments:

> These otherworldly religious ideals ["the way that the world ought to be"]—for Buddhists, the idea of karma—drive the institutions into different mission orientation in this world. How these mission ideals practically materialize will depend upon social realities, such as the institution's resources and strategies and the reception of the community at large.[80]

Frederick Jackson Turner's notion that *communitas* as the soul of ritual is reflected here. Asian American communities such as the Dharma Light Temple belong to a different logical category. It is "an essential and generic human bond, without which there could be no society."[81] Community for Asian Americans, in other words, is not itself a part of social structure but is one of society's reasons for being. Since *communitas* transcends empirical categories and has to be comprehended in a subjunctive rather than an indicative mode, that is, as a potentiality, it

---

79. Jeung, *Faithful Generations*, 237.
80. Chen, "Cultivating Acceptance by Cultivating Merit," 80.
81. Turner, *The Ritual Process*, 83.

is absent and present at any time, hence it is liminal, existing in between logical categories. It lives by ritual.

The liminality of rituals means that they are informed, on the one hand, by a greater than usual sense of order and, on the other hand, by a heightened sense of freedom and possibility. For a privileged group, dream of a common humanity, especially when ritualized and therefore brought into experience, can threaten a socially privileged way of life. It is different among the exploited and the marginalized. When a spirit of rebellion against unjust social structure is rising, an understanding of ritual as an alternative order fostering freedom, creativity, and deliverance will take precedence over the idea that rituals enforce rigid notions of order. Ritual will be seen as the occasion for both symbolizing and experiencing relationships in which spontaneity, affection, and unity replace unwanted law and compelled obedience. Under these conditions, communities will put ritual in the service of personal and social transformation.

"Indeed, new communities—Asian American pan-ethnic ones—have been born. The bazaar has become a pan-ethnic tradition used as a means to understand how God builds solidarity among a new community of people," says Russell Jeung.[82] Ritual not only brings people together in physical assembly but also functions to unite them emotionally and spiritually. It bonds people in even deeper ways. This aspect of ritual is related to the liminal nature of the spirit of dissonance and dissent.

Charles Long's notion that the historiography of the disfranchised to recover their own identities through their own narratives as "'crawling back' through one's history" speaks of Asian American spirit of dissonance and dissent to a certain extent.[83] However, an act of "crawling back" is diffuse, shifting, and often contradictory. The Asian Americans' role and contributions to the *actus tradendi* of its own is thus "crawling back" to our histories through our own narrative descriptions of our subjectivity by "stumbling and stuttering" guided by the spirit of dissonant and dissent. Given the Foucault's notion of power imbalance implied in the tradition-making (his description of "genealogy"), our own subjectivity claim and our insistence in writing our own history is indeed is a way of what Friedrich Nietzsche call "someone coming into being,. . . again and again [reality] reinterpreted to new ends, taken over,

---

82. Jeung, *Faithful Generations*, 238.
83. Long, *Significations*, 9.

transformed, and redirected by some power superior to it."[84] That "some power" is not transcendent of our own powers. Rather, it is the power that arises out of the whole of Asian American collectivity that is more than a sum of each part. The diaspolic life of Asian Americans even in a seemingly stable and secure environment of the contemporary U.S. is in fact tumultuous and dissonant to one's own self-understanding once understood from within. Tradition-building in such a world of dissonance and dissent is lived and reflected within this vicissitudious context by Asian Americans. It is part and parcel of a wider life experience and its driving spirit, and it cannot be understood otherwise. *Actus tradendi* in this context is, in a large measure, an attempt to uncover hidden insights into meaning making, and to trace their dispersion through the domain of social, cultural, and political practices, thus bringing into play their full subversive role. Reflective activity thus does not seek to make the opaque insights into faith transparent to the dominant constituencies, rather seeks through the avenues of our own subjectivity claim to empower the opaque in the quest of representation and freedom. The question before us is what "dangerous memories" and insights are brought into the traditioning genealogy of faith and meaning making by Asian translocal communities in America.

---

84. Nietzsche, *On the Genealogy of Morals*, 77.

4

Amphibolous Faith

Reality Is Multiple

To summarize the discussion of this work so far, we began with the notion of a "second language" as a way of speaking of American peoplehood whichthat holds people together along with the first language of democracy. A "second language" grows out of an alternate "storied site," that is, in the story shaped in a particular community of disfranchised people, where lost memories are recovered, buried histories are retraced, silence emerges in an articulated fashion, and fractured relationships with neighbors are reestablished. A "second language" is the "language of tradition and commitment in a community of memory" of people who have lived particularly in the fringe of our society, to paraphrase the expression of sociologist Robert Bellah. On the one hand, our interpretation of peoplehood has its referential sources both in the river of a myriad of representative historical interpretations of people that have existed in the margin of our society and, on the other, a particular epistemological locus in which the interpreter is situated, a locus from which the distinctness of Asian Americans' shared story is analyzed. The framework of the interpretation is the epistemological scaffold based on the lived experiences of Americans of the Asian descent. The scaffold is threefold: the translocal life embedded in a racialized community with a specific set of value orientations; a diasporic identity that is dissonant with the prevailing societal norms fostering a heightened sensitivity toward pathos in life; and thirdly a particular faith orientation that is an "amphibolous" or hybrid negotiation among myriad faith traditions and cosmologies that Asian Americans inhereted. These three pillars constitute Asian American epistemology. They are critical in analyzing Asian American experiences. These epistemological pillars shape the contour of this interpretation of American peoplehood.

The first pillar of the three-fold epistemological scaffold is translocality and ruptural liminality associated with our experiences of race. Asian Americans are racially translocal. We are a "People on the Way." Race experienced as translocality results from an unresolved tension that exists among divergent sets of understandings of who Asian Americans are, the tension consisting of the rupture between an internal racial awareness and an externally imposed identity. The internal self-awareness of race takes the expression of a multiple consciousness akin to what W. E. B. Du Bois calls "the veil" or "double consciousness," "two warring souls, two thoughts, two unreconciled strivings; two warring ideals in one dark body, whose dogged strength alone keeps it from being torn asunder."[1] For Asian Americans the "veil" exists at the level of multiple consciousness, not merely bipolar. Externally, race as translocality is situated at the intersection of the contrasting images imposed by the society of a "foreigner within" on the one hand and a "model minority" on the other. Translocality also results from racially induced "rupturally liminal" experiences, both historically and at the present time. Asian Americans experience race as "ruptural," unexpected occurrence that intrudes into life, and the normalcy of life suddenly disrupted without prior warning. It is a rupture caused by decisions made outside of their control, such as the Chinese Exclusion Act in the 19th century, the Internment of Japanese Americans during World War II, and more recently the racial profiling of Arab and South Asian Americans. These experiences are "liminal" because Asian Americans are forced to negotiate externally imposed decisions that affect our lives and our own self-understanding of who we are at the same time. This rupturally liminal experience of translocality of is the "continuing material contradictions" of race according to Lisa Lowe, the locus where our collective identities and values are forged and claimed.[2] The translocal experiences of race thus create a nomadic value orientation of "not being at home in one's own home," as Theodore Adorno puts it.[3]

---

1. Du Bois, *The Souls of Black Folk*, 9..
2. Lowe, *Immigrant Acts*.
3. Adorno, Quoted in Said, *Reflections on Exile*, 184.

The second pillar of the Asian American epistemological scaffold is the sensitivity to pathos, that is, also the spirit of dissonance and dissent. A translocal person's identity and values are often dissonant with the prevailing societal and dominant cultural milieu of America. In the context of such dissonance a "local cultural originality" (Franz Fanon) is difficult to achieve. Moreover the dissonance Asian Americans experience derives not only from the translocal experiences of race but equally from the memory of woundedness, both injuries experienced collectively in history and the woundedness that is very much alive in our own lives today, thereby making us particularly disposed to the pathos that accompanies life. This heightened sensitivity toward pathos in life originates from Asian Americans' experiences of the incongruence between, on the one hand, the publicly stated ideal of the democratic nation in which Asian Americans live, the notion of life, liberty and the pursuit of happiness, and on the other hand, from our own experiences of suffering, injustice, and exclusion from the ideal of what America is proclaimed to be. Furthermore, the sensitivity to pathos is, at the same time, a spirit of protest against the privileged and blindly optimistic reading of life that devalues the pathos that is prevalent in this "officially optimistic society."[4] As in the case of those Japanese Americans who fought proudly for the very nation that feared them during World War II and who forgave America's toxic forgetfulness and the treatment of supposed strangers without forgetting it, this dissenting spirit critiques the toxicity that accompanies the dominant outlook of life embedded in politics, consumptive economics, education, and the landscape of the organized religions.[5] The spirit of dissonance and dissent originates in the nagging sense of "not really fitting in" America today and critiques the society that treats difference as "less-than" in an adversarial and oppositional fashion.

This spirit of dissonance and dissent is expressed as a heightened sensitivity toward the plight of other dislocated and dismissed people who "have rights but are incapable of imposing these interests or these rights," As George Semeaan puts it.[6] Asian Americans have developed this spirit of dissonance and dissent out of our own experiences of dis-

---

4. The term an "officially optimistic society" originates from Hall, *Lighten Our Darkness*.

5. Ibid.

6. Semaan, quoted in Wall, "Eyes to See," 45.

cordance with the cosmologies, worldviews, ideologies, and organized religions that are rooted in the North Atlantic orientation of life. To be sure, the spirit of dissonance and dissent is not exclusive to Asian American communities. Increasingly this spirit exists in many quarters both in American and abroad. Edward Said's description of exilic communities is exemplary in this regard. The queering perspectives that are emerging in trans-gender and trans-sexual communities are another example. Whenever people are in a state of disruption and displacement, the spirit of dissonance and dissent is likely to emerge in their communities. Among Asian Americans this spirit is embodied in improvisational rituals expressed within our communities, particularly in our faith communities. The spirit lives in the stories they tell of their tormented history, and the stories are repeated as often as necessary. The message of Said that emerges out of this discordant spirit is this: by embracing this spirit of dissonance and dissent more openly, albeit with due respect, the American society just may be able to grasp the reality and experiences of those who exist in an underside of life, both in our own society and in a wider world. Without acknowledging this alternate social convention, Americans will remain uncritically committed to the prevailing values of stability, security, and optimism expressed in the truncated notion of democratic freedom. Freedom has become an entitlement only resulted from an act of excluding those who live outside of these values, tragically repeating over and over again an uncritical affirmation of "life, liberty and the pursuit of happiness" as the accepted canon of the land.

AMPHIBOLOUS FAITH: NON-SINGULAR VISION OF THE WEB OF RELATIONSHIPS

The challenge facing the privileged American population is a rehabilitation of a relationship-building with alienated groups of people both at home and abroad. The renewal of peoplehood is contrapuntal (Edward Said), that is, viewing the reality of an interconnected web of life as an ensemble of disparate choices and priorities that make up the whole material and spiritual world. "With the lives of the diverse characters starkly juxtaposed—in constant counterpoint . . . creates a world that offers both biting criticism and profound sympathy" at the same time, says Said..[7] Such a contrapuntal task for the renewal of peoplehood seeks a mutual consideration of otherwise seemingly incongruent second languages that express social practices, of culture, of history, with particular attention given to the practices, culture, history and religiosity of certain communities of people that have been historically undervalued.[8] In other words, attention needs to be paid to otherwise neglected pieces in order to see a whole picture. The angle of vision that addresses this contrapuntal and non-singular life-orientation is the third pillar of the Asian American epistemological scaffold, *amphibolous faith* of. The term amphibolous faith is really a theological expression embedded particularly within Asian American Christian communities though it operates in other faith communities as well. Amphibolous faith supplements or complements the first two epistemological pillars, i.e., our translocal racialized existence and the spirit of dissonance and dissent. The three pillars stand together, mutually supporting the function of the others in the formation of the communal coherence of Asian Americans.

This third pillar, amphibolous faith, challenges the epistemological foundation of the nationhood of America, *e pluribus unum*, "one out of many," and offers an alternate foundation, "reality is multiple." Jacques Derrida uses the term *"plus d'Un"* to a great effect to explain this notion of reality being multiple. In French language *"plus d'Un"* means "the more than One," but it also means "one no more" or "no longer One." What's at stake with *d'Un* is that the assumed One is actually multiple. Perhaps even a multiple that somehow relates as one, but certainly we must drop the capital "O" of One, leaving us with one+one, at least. Derrida uses *plus d'Un* to suggest that we are always already dealing with a division at the heart of things (such as nations or communities) that produces pluralism or at least multiplicity.[9]

How does Derrida's term *"plus d'Un"* help explain amphibolous faith practiced and lived in Asian American communities? "Amphiboly" is the simultaneous existence of radically different epistemological and cosmological orientations in a person or in a community, the orientations that are materially expressed as well as spiritually lived. Furthermore, the contradiction of these orientations does not readily settle for a resolution or compromise. Amphibolous faith arises particularly within the

---

7. Said, *Huxley's Point Counter Point*.
8. Said, *Culture and Imperialism*, 36.
9. Derrida, *La Religion*, 65.

lives of those who navigate the chasm between the historic and material dominance of the Hellenistic metaphysical reading of radical monotheism embedded in Christianity on the one hand and the often non-theistic and ontological orientations derived from the Asian religions and cosmologies on the other. Amphibolous faith does not replace one faith with another in a binary fashion. Amphibolous faith adds another faith to an existing one even in contradiction. Amphibolous faith is a way of thinking, living through, and interpreting together experiences that are discordant, each with its own integrity, pace of development, internal formations and systems of external relationships, all co-existing and interacting with each other critically within one's existence both individually and communally.

Furthermore, amphibolous faith does not mean a relativistic "wishy-washy" spirituality in which indecision and non-commitment are the primary posture. In the midst of separation, displacement, and *differend*, there is a mingling of involvements and detachments that is a transaction of connection.[10] Because a person who embraces amphibolous faith sees reality both in terms of what has been left behind, or what could have been, and what is actual, here and now, there is a multiple perspective that doesn't see things in isolation or in binary relationship. In other words, amphiboly is an experience of a "non-singular vision" with an unresolved state of non-complimentary cosmologies and faith traditions simultaneously existing within a person.

Furthermore, the epistemology of amphiboly has its own *telos*. Amphiboly aims most of all to express the "unnegotiability" of the web of relationships, interpersonally or as a community. What is at stake in such a non-singular vision of life is the priority of values placed upon connectivity and a web of existence in multiplicity. What is at stake in amphibolous faith is an *a priori* longing for relationship-building, not a binary construction of oppositional dynamics in human relationships, a longing that is yet to be realized. Amphibolous faith often takes the ex-

---

10. Lyotard defines a *differend* as "a case of conflict, between (at least) two parties, that cannot be equitably resolved for lack of a rule of judgment applicable to both arguments." (*The Differend,* xi). Conflicts can arise when people are engaged in discourses that are incommensurable. Because there are no rules that apply across discourses, the conflicts become *differends*. To enforce a rule in a *differend* is to enforce the role of one discourse or the other, resulting in a wrong suffered by the party whose rule of discourse is ignored.

pression of noncompetitive and organic connections among contrasting and often contradictory religious and cosmological orientations.

Amphibolous faith often takes on diverse expressions in Asian American communities. It is equally present both in immigrant communities as well as in communities that are deeply rooted in the American soil. The examples described below are those of recent immigrant communities. A "critical faith," a "new civil religion" for Japanese Americans described by Jane Iwamura, is another expression of an amphibolous faith.[11]

> In an important sense, Japanese American Civil Religion remains in constant dialogue with its American counterpart—sharing much of its language and principles. But the texts, sites, and rituals that inform its stance remain historically unique. They are also influenced by religious and cultural traditions and ways of engaging the world that differ from the religious patterns of Christianity and Roman Republicanism that undergird American civil religion. Attention to these traditions and spiritual sensibilities are key to fully understanding the distinctiveness of Japanese American civil religious formation and the spirit that sustains its vision.[12]

Among the expressions of Japanese American civil religions a notable example is the Manzanar Pilgrimage, the site of a Japanese American internment camp during World War II, and Day of Remembrance, and an annual commemorative event of the internment at Manzanar, California and other camp sites. Through participation in the pilgrimage and memorial services, theologian Joanne Doi say, "Japanese American religious subjects perform and embody this worldview (a sense of the group—whether family, workplace, or nation—) is inextricably tied to the value and worth of each individual as they both remember those loved ones who have passed away *and* reaffirm their ancestors and ultimately themselves as part of a larger network."[13] This new civil religion is amphibolous because it exists within the larger framework of what Robert Bellah calls America's civil religion.[14] No matter what expressions an amphibolous faith takes, it is likely contrapuntal and a "critical"

---

11. Iwamura, "Critical Faith," 937f.
12. Ibid., 955.
13. Ibid., 958.
14. Bellah, *The Broken Covenant*.

reading of reality. An amphibolous faith remains in constant conversation with its American counterpart, democratic freedom, as it has come to be understood at this early phase of the 21st century. It is embedded in both civil and religious communities where race, ethnicity, and faith merge to create a sphere of moral commitment and concern. Perhaps, it is more accurate to say that a dichotomy between civil practices and religiosity does not really exist in amphibolous living.

Another example of amphibolous faith comes from a Cambodian American family. Describing the story of tragedy experienced by a Cambodian American family in Stockton, California, in 1989, Asian American news reporter Katherine Kam gives testimony to a particular expression of amphibolous faith. This story illustrates the unnegotiability of the well of relationships embedded in an amphibolous expression of faith by Asian Americans. Kam, a freelance journalist, describes how the Chun family lived through an amphibolous faith.[15] The story also reveals how the particular Cambodian American family, Chuns, and their practice of faith challenges the normativity and canon of the Abrahamic monotheistic cosmology prevalent in North America. The story also speaks of the practice of faith as it relates to claims for the subjectivity of this Cambodian American family amidst the material contradictions of race, gender, class, and a diasporic life.

The story begins with a school shooting in which a young white drifter with a history of mental problems vented his rage upon 400 schoolchildren at Cleveland Elementary School in Stockton before shooting himself through the head. Among the dead were four Cambodian American children, one Vietnamese; the majority of the 29 injured students were Americans of Southeast Asian descent. Keut Chun and his spouse, Im Chun, lost their eight-year-old daughter, Ram, in the tragic incident. This traumatic experience brought back painful memories for the Keut and Im Chun, the beatings and hard labor they enduredsuffered in Khmer Rouge camps in Cambodia. Sadly, they lost more than fifty relatives under the Pol Pot regime before they escaped to a Thai refugee camp where Ram was born. Following the tragic incident of Cleveland Elementary School, Keut Chun began a daily ritual.

Following the shooting, the Chuns and other Southeast Asian Americans in Stockton reported mental flashbacks of past horrors in Cambodia, sleeplessness, lack of appetite, hallucinations, withdrawal,

---

15. Kam, "False and Shattered Peace," 8–21.

anxiety and depression. Unfamiliar with Western medicine, one Cambodian American woman feared that upon release from the hospital, "her injured son would die under her care at home."[16] Funeral arrangements for Ram not only increased the sense of hopelessness but also an additional confusion. The Asian American families wanted a customary large and elaborate ceremony, a symbol of healing and transition. The funeral home, on the other hand, was accustomed to small, somber, Western-style funerals. Furthermore, the Buddhist families were afraid that a Buddhist ceremony with cremation—rather than a Christian funeral with burial—would offend the rest of the American community. The legally required autopsies also upset parents, particularly the Buddhists, who believed that cutting the bodies would interfere with the proper process of reincarnation. California law also prevented the parents from taking the bodies of their children home to prepare them for burial, their customary practice in their native countries.

Following the tragic incident, there was an onslaught of support and media attention:

> [S]ix days after the shooting, the Chuns, the Lims and other families felt honored and comforted when dignitaries such as the Superintendent of Schools Bill Honig, Governor George Deukmejian and state Attorney General John Van de Kamp joined more than 3,000 mourners of all colors in a Buddhist-Christian service at the city's civic auditorium. Each slain child was remembered with a minute of silence. Sokhim An. Ram Chun. Oeun Lim. Rathanar Or. Thuy Tran. Later Sokhim and Ram, best friends in life, were buried side by side.[17]

The school and county health agencies extended their resources as much as they can to help the surviving students, parents, and families cope with the trauma. But the help both overwhelmed the Southeast Asian American communities and failed to address the real needs of the families. For one thing, the whole concept of mental health was foreign to them and their exigent needs were expressed in cultural and religious forms uniquely tied to their Southeast Asian American experience.

Illustrating the disconnect between the suffering Asian American families and the broader local community of Stockton, when the news of Ram's death reached the Chuns' relatives in Dallas, Texas, where the

---

16. Ibid., 8.
17. Ibid., 11.

Chuns once lived when they first came to the U.S., they contacted pastor Sophal Ung, a Cambodian American Christian pastor in Stockton, and asked him to help the Chun family.

> Like the Chuns, Southeast Asian families affected by the tragedy turned to religious leaders after the shooting. Two of the dead children were Buddhist, three Christian. In Stockton, free flow and friendship exist between the two bodies of believers, despite theological differences. Ung's church had sponsored the Chuns in the U.S. Like them, Ung knows tragedy first-hand . . . The Chuns attend church with Ung, who also visits them regularly. A month after the shooting, a vivid dream pierced Im Chun's nightmares. She told Ung she saw her slain daughter "living with God in heaven. She was wearing a white dress, clapping her hands and smiling down at me."[18]

The Chuns trusted Pastor Ung because of their mutually shared backgrounds. Keut and Im both come from a culture influenced by strong Confucian ethics that emphasize coping, family stability, maintaining personal dignity and the dignity of one's family. They were fearful of losing face by exposing problems to outsiders other than village elders or religious leaders. "If I know someone, I will tell him everything in my heart . . . If I don't know him, I will say nothing."[19]

Other families of injured and slain children sought comfort from Dharmawara Mahathera, a high-ranking, a 100-year-old monk regarded as the spiritual leader of Stockton's Cambodian Buddhists.

> The families don't say much when they come. They ask "Bhante," as the monk is respectfully addressed by his followers, to chant mantras over them and to meditate with him. About one month after the shooting, a little boy whose sister died at Cleveland began crying uncontrollably because he thought he had seen a vision of the girl dancing before his eyes. His parents brought him to Dharmawara, whose prayers calmed the children down.[20]

Further illustrating the disjunction between the prevailing values of the surrounding community and those of the Southeast Asian Americans affected by the slayings, Dharmawara considered the mental health services offered to the families to be an overreaction that under-

---

18. Ibid.
19. Ibid.
20. Ibid.

estimated the families' ability to cope with their grief. "Priests go deeper into the hearts and minds of the hearer . . . This matter concerns the mind. It concerns spirituality. I don't think any crude remedy will solve the problem. Prayer is enough."[21]

Following the incident at Cleveland School, the Chuns faced an uncertain future. Their family life was profoundly affected by the incident. Their sixteen-year-old son, Rann, increasingly challenged the authority of his parents and was caught fighting at school. The Chuns turned to Ung and other trusted Cambodian church leaders for help with their son.

> Chun seems resigned to his fate . . . "I am already old," he says. "When I came here, I wanted my children to grow up to be good, to have good educations, to be doctors or teachers, to have a better life in this country. There is hope for the children. Already, Rann Chun has grown a little less fearful of going into the bathroom alone. But in the living room, his father continues to watch the videotape of Ram's funeral day after day. Pallbearers march across the screen carrying coffins mounted with huge photographs of the youngsters. Mourners chant prayers in Cambodian. Keut Chun lowers his head as his eyes mist. "I will never believe my daughter is dead."[22]

In the absence of a familiar ritual practice for such an occasion in an unfamiliar land, Keut Chun created a ritual of his own that helped him cope with the tragedy that befell him and his family. He played back the videotape of the funeral service every morning. "In a corner of a sparsely furnished living room, Keut Chun, a frail man bundled into a heavy jacket, sits on a floor mat and watches a videotape of the funeral for his daughter, Ram... . . .. Im Chan says her husband has watched the videotape every day since their daughter was buried two months earlier."[23] In this ritual he concocted himself, reliving the funeral through the medium of videotape, the familiar words of Cambodian prayers are placed within the context of the new land. The traditional expressions of grief co-mingle with the improvisational and make-shift form of the Buddhist-Christian funeral, providing Keut Chun an amphibolous expression of faith practice that is distinct from any familiar traditional

21. Ibid.
22. Ibid.
23. Ibid., 8.

faith practices. This improvised practice kept Keut Chun in touch with his daughter whom he did not believe was dead. Even with an absence of familiar spiritual surroundings, Keut Chun was able to make do with a combination of different religious traditions, thereby creating an amphibolous space in which—provisionally at least—he could grieve and connect with his daughter. Playing the videotape of Ram's funeral, Keut Chun was able to "re-remember" with her, since memory is not only an activity of the mind but also of the body, including the bodies and minds of others with whom his life was interwoven and interconnected.

Such an amphibolous space created by improvisational ritual plays an important role in the preservation of memory, as it involves the active bodily participation of all those who are present both in the past and the present. In this case, through improvisational ritual all lives affected by the senseless tragic event resulting in the death of Chun's daughter are reconnected, thus affirming the *apiori* "unnegotiable" web of relationships. The improvised ritual for Keut Chun is a movement towards the center of the web of life, the source of the social-moral order of the cosmos, even as Chun attempts to navigate the unfamiliar terrain of the surrounding chaos of the American society in which he finds himself. The daily ritual of re-playing the video tape of his daughter's funeral is his attempt to regain his center as a communal person by reconnecting to his history and to his daughter, to his family, and to his community, all of which areexist in the periphery of American society. In this way, the ritual is a journey, a sacred journey, even to his own otherness in the strange land that brings him home to himself. It is not an escape from but a return to the center of his fragmented history, to the pivotal events that mark him as a person of amphibolous faith. In a paradoxical way, the center of his history—including the priority placed upon a web of relationships, albeit located on the margin of society—recreates and revitalizes the web itself.

REALITY IS MULTIPLE: THE GRAMMAR THAT DEFIES A CONVENTIONAL ARTICULATION OF "ONE IN MANY"

In the novel by Yoshiko Uchida, *Picture Bride*, the words of the main character, Kiku, also reveal the complexity of amphibolous faith. "'I guess

I'm part-Buddhist, part-Christian and part nothing at all,' she laughed."[24] Kiku's words do not merely indicate the state of her spiritual confusion. Her words express the unresolved state of her material life, her gradual realization that she is indeed a translocal person and that she has left the stability and familiarity of her home, Japan. She longs for security and yet also is aware that security and stability are not to be had in America. Kiku longs for a sense of belonging amidst the dislocation of her life in America. "'I guess I'm part-Buddhist, part-Christian and part nothing at all,' she laughed," expresses the unfamiliar amphibolous terrain of her existence in both words and an apparently embarrassed laughter. In her inarticulate expression, Kiku intuitively affirms that reality is indeed multiple, not to be reduced to the singularity of the "unity in diversity" or a binary "either-or" paradigm. She also refuses to be "interpellated" into the powerful forces of Christian monotheism, the dominant western cultural mode of America.[25] What is interpellation?

Theresa Hak Kyung Cha's book *Dictee* describes the grammar of amphiboly and affirms the epistemological foundation of reality's multiplicity through her critique of "interpellation." She does so by focusing on the forces of interpellation powerfully operating within American society. In the section "Calliope," written from the perspective of a Korean American woman returning to South Korea for a visit, the narrator recalls her naturalization into the United States. The maintenance of her language, history, national origin, race, and gender are at odds with assimilation, the latter being an amphibolous compromising process ultimately promising U.S. citizenship. Her identity and subjectivity are "multiply determined but also that each determination is uneven and historically differentiated, leaving a variety of residues that remain uncontained by and antagonistic to the educational, religious, colonial, and imperial modes of domination and assimilation," says Lisa Lowe as she interprets this story.[26] The narrator describes her displaced situation as a Korean American immigrant in a visit to her place of origin:

> Eighteen years pass. I am here for the first time in eighteen years, Mother. We left here in this memory still fresh, still new. I speak another tongue, a second tongue. This is how distant I am. From

---

24. Uchida, *Picture Bride*, 13.

25. The term "interpellation" was originally used by Althusser and is explained below.

26. Lowe, *Immigrant Acts*, 52.

> then. From that time. They take me back they have taken me back so precisely now exact to the hour to the day to the season in the smoke mist in the drizzle I turn the corner and there is no one. No one facing me. The street is rubble. I put my palm on my eyes to rub them, then I let them cry freely. Two school children with their book bags appear from nowhere with their arms around each other. Their white kerchief, their white shirt uniform, into a white residue of gas, crying.[27]

Her pathos is the loss of contact with the solidity and the satisfaction of earth, a true homecoming out of the question: "They take me back they have taken me back so precisely now exact to the hour to the day to the season in the smoke mist in the drizzle . . . ." And yet, when she turns the corner, " . . . there is no one. No one facing me. The street is rubble." Still, in such a state of displacement and loss there exists a real drive for life, crying "freely." The tears well up out of her life. The two children with their arms around each other, in a white residue of gas, cry and dissolve seamlessly between "life and death." The narrator refuses to acquiesce to the official account of the event that privileges insurgencies, containments, and violence central to both U.S. neocolonialism and South Korean nationalism. But in claiming her own agency she is also aware of the simultaneous existence of the irresolution of her painful historical past and her yearning for restoration and wholeness. This is amphiboly. Her experience connotes an acknowledgement and acceptance of the givenness of such a disparity between relationship and the sense of loss. The oppressive state of life is not to be essentialized, as it exists in the highly charged historical circumstances of the material construction of life. Simone Weil reminds us that to be rooted in a particular place is perhaps the most important and least recognized need of the human soul, so to exist in a state of amphiboly could result in the resentment of those who live in material security and rootedness. On the other hand, living with amphiboly also offers anthe opportunity to affirm life's meaning within a state of disparity and instability. That is why an amphibolous existence is "sacred," suggestive of the mystery of the depth of life. To be sure, to live in a state of amphiboly very well may promote jealousy, a longing for that which cannot be had.

And yet, the unattainability of security and rootedness is precisely the source of life, the reservoir of its vitality. The truth of faith in such a

---

27. Cha, *Dictee*, 85.

state is not an objectively verifiable ahistorical matter but is something that is wrestled over in the midst of daily life. In the familiar conventional grammar of faith, convictions are reinforced by invoking received authorities, sacred texts, exemplary achievements, and generally accepted benchmarks. At the same time, there always lurks in any conviction an element of doubt that can negate assurance, permanence, and certainty. And yet, one yearns for an intimate relationship with others even in such a state. One craves a rehabilitative relatedness even in the actual state of fractured and fragmented life. In this state truth is acknowledged not as a result of indubitable proof but as a result of the very real power of rhetoric. This is the grammar of amphiboly.

In order to analyze the interpenetration of divergent cosmologies in the practices of faith of Asian Americans, we must recognize that what Louis Althusser calls *interpellation* is at work even in entrenched communities of Asian Americans.[28] "Interpellation," according to Althusser, is the process through which subjects internalize ideologies that recruit them as speakers or authors.[29] For example, "It is for you that I have shed my blood" is an interpellative statement. By becoming a recipient of the sacrifice, a person becomes an advocate and a spokesperson for the initiator of the statement and his ideological position. Interpellation suggests that ideologies function through the subject, though it is defined as not accounting for the totality of subjective practice. Interpellation contains something akin to the psychoanalytic notion of splitting, but whereas psychoanalysis figures this splitting metaphorically as the "castration" of the subject upon entering language and social relations already existing in a given society, in interpellation this division is figured otherwise as a tension between the ideological demand for identification and the contradictory material conditions within which the demand is made. This is to say, interpellation is inherently contradictory. A newly emerging cosmological orientation of Asian American Christians, represented by Kiku in *Picture Bride* and the narrator of *Dictee*, reflects the interpellative forces operating as much within Asian Christian communities as within the wider American society. At the same time, contradictory and subversive attempts are also made in the midst of the interpellative forces by such Asian American Christians. In a scene describing a visit

---

28. Lowe, *Immigrant Acts*, 145.
29. Althusser, "Ideology and Ideological State Apparatuses," in *For Marx*.

to a Catholic church for confession, Theresa Cha portrays the powerful interpellative forces operating:

> I am making up the sins. For the guarantee of absolution. In the beginning again, at zero. Before Heaven even. Before the Fall. All previous wrongs erased. Reduced to spotless. Pure . . . To make words. To make a speech in such tongues.
>
> Q: WHO MADE THEE?
>
> A: God made me.
>
> To conspire in God's tongue.
>
> Q: WHERE IS GOD?
>
> A: God is everywhere.
>
> Accomplice in His Texts, the fabrication in His Own Image, the pleasure the desire of giving
>
> Image to the world in the mind of the confessor.
>
> Q: GOD WHO HAS MADE YOU IN HIS OWN LIKENESS.
>
> A: God who made me in His own likeness.
>
> In His Own Image in His Own Resemblance, in
>
> His Own Copy, In His Own Counterfeit Presentment, in His Duplicate, in His Own Reproduction, in His Cast, in His Carbon . . . Acquiesce, to the correspondence. Acquiesce, to the messenger. Acquiesce to and for the complot in the Hieratic tongue . . . Theirs. Into Their tongue, the counterscript, my confession in Theirs. Into Theirs. To scribe to make hear the words, to make sound the words, the words, the words made flesh.[30]

The interpellation that takes place in *Dictee* is "a subordination of the multiple to the identical" in the name of faith, that is, the familiar notion of "one in many," *e pluribus unum*.[31] The creation of human beings in the divine image is here interpreted as "constructed imaginary equivalences of identification" while the material site of struggle is kept unchallenged: "that identification involves a continual, repressed recognition of differentiation."[32] To interpellate the material contradictions of

---

30. Cha, *Dictee*, 16–19.
31. Lowe, *Immigrant Acts*, 148.
32. Ibid., 151.

differentiation, Theresa Cha argues in *Dictee* for the recognition of the irresolution of contradictions. Only then, in this act of recognition of "holy irresolution," does one's own subjectivity claim become possible and its authenticity legitimized. While interpellation is a reality particularly within Asian American Christian faith communities, their amphibolous existence and spiritual orientation place the communities in a critical distance from raw interpellative forces. In contrast to the forces in American society that speak of the "one out of many," an amphibolous orientation affirms that reality is indeed multiple, "*plus d'Un.*"

Another example of an amphibolous faith countering interpellative forces in America comes from a Japanese American Protestant congregation in northern California. Responding to the pastor's question directed to the congregation during a Sunday morning sermon at Sycamore Congregational Church in El Cerrito, California, "Do you love Jesus?," a *Nisei* (a second-generation Japanese American) member quietly murmured: "Maybe, maybe not." This comment might be taken as a comical expression tinged with embarrassment in this generally non-evangelical group of Japanese American Christians. On the contrary, this comment instantiates a genuinely honest expression of the amphibolous faith understanding and grammar of an Asian American. It is also a powerful dissent against the interpellative forces at work in Asian American Christianity.

TTo cite another example of the absence of conflicted and contradictory dualism in the life of Sycamore Congregational is also described by former Japanese-languagespeaking Pastor Mitsuho Okado. Pastor Okado observes that the whole definition of Christian identity and corresponding rituals such as baptism and the Eucharist need to be re-examined in Asian American Christian congregations in light of the emerging changes in the composition of the congregation.[33] Those members of Sycamore congregation who come out of religious traditions other than Christianity tend to begin actively participating in Sycamore church and its programs through — their children's entrance into the church-sponsored preschool. For these participants —the definition of what constitutes the church's "membership" has been called into question. Does a "member" mean a baptized person who confesses her/his faithfulness to the Christian faith? How would the church respond to a person who is willing to say that she/he is a "Christian" because

---

33. Okado, "A Challenge of Re-forming a Community."

that person is very active in the church and yet is not baptized? If these participants are classified as "non-members," what message would the designation convey to them and to the whole church, which ostensibly values inclusivity and community-building? These questions become serious issues for the church when the "official" members comprise a relatively small percentage of those who are truly active in the church programs. Pastor Okado observes:

> It is Sycamore's [Congregational Church] challenge to form one body [that includes] new immigrants who might be known as "weaker" (1 Corinthians 2) or a new participant. By forming, re-forming and redefining a community with them Sycamore will have the image of the community as a whole. This is the process of forming a community with *issei* [new participants] who seem to be weaker [a new member] and in this process Sycamore can achieve its own mission as a Japanese American Church.[34]

By the use of the term "weaker" participants, Pastor Okado means those who participate in various church activities but nevertheless do not consider themselves to be an official member of the congregation because of their non-baptized status while, at the same time, considering themselves to be a "Christian" and full and active participant in the congregation. Okado argues that the traditional notion of baptism as a necessary means for membership needs to be re-examined in light of those active participants in the congregation who do not wish to be baptized.

> Though baptism is sociologically considered as a necessary "qualification" [for church membership,] we need to remember that it is theologically a sacrament. That is to say that those who belong to the faith community need the divine guidance that is beyond human activities. The work of the church is to actualize God's work. Therefore, baptism is not merely the matter of the relationship between Christ and the faithful (one Spirit, one body, I Corinthians. 12:13) but should be considered as a ritual of the church. The church's responsibility is to form a community that is harmonious of those who gather with diverse religious backgrounds. In this process of the community formation we find the true nature of the church.[35]

---

34. Ibid., viii.
35. Ibid., 138. The translation from Japanese provided by the author of this work.

> The Japanese-speaking members of the church considered the establishment of the preschool as a means for the church's evangelism and mission. It was difficult for them to reconcile the large number of attendance in the preschool related activities and a small number of attendees at Sunday morning worship service. The reason for their disappointment lies in the church's lack of understanding in the religiosity of Japanese. Namely, the church confused the community-belonging with a narrowly defined membership. Furthermore, the church lost the sight of baptism as a sacrament . . . As the preschool celebrates its tenth anniversary, Sycamore Congregational Church is realizing the meaning of its outreach into the local community and of its own existence.[36]

The meaning of baptism is thus re-examined in this context and its theological meaning reinterpreted as an amphibolous dimension of the community. These narratives of actual life of faith speak of the improvisational and anti-interpellative practices and rituals that go on within Asian American faith communities. These practices and rituals produce a Christian theology that is often radically different from what has been considered normative in Christian history. These practices and rituals, furthermore, question and contradict the fundamental premise of an Abrahamic faith cosmology, that is, the primacy and normativity of a monotheistic divine initiative and revelation in all that exists. The monotheistic cosmology of Christian faith is placed on an equal par by the "members" of Sycamore congregation with other cosmologies that are inherited from Asia and are mutated into a new expression in the actual Christian faith practices of Asian Americans.

These phenomena are different from the familiar notion of syncretism that still implies the normativeness of the monotheistic cosmology of the Abrahamic faith of Christianity. The conventional notion of "syncretism" presupposes non-Christian worldviews and faith traditions are incorporated into the presumed Christian norm. In the faith practices of Asian Americans no privileged differential exists between the traditional Christian monotheism and other faith orientations. The differing cosmologies are co-equal. Furthermore, these cosmologies and worldviews continue to evolve in the practices of Asian American communities creating hybridized and distinct cosmological and religious expressions of their own, amphiboly, in the midst of our struggle to claim one's own subjectivity in a racially hybridized and translocal

36. Ibid., 126–27.

life. Furthermore, these new expressions of faith call into question the historically assumed narratives of religion, migration and settlement in the United States based on "radical monotheism."[37] Thus they suggest the emergence of an alternate way of defining "peoplehood."

To be sure, traditional "Christian" expressions of faith still prevail among many Asian Americans. Nevertheless, the interpenetration of divergent religious traditions and practices and the improvisation of rituals in Asian American communities are increasingly common phenomena. Reflecting on religion and spirituality in Korean America, historian David K. Yoo and Ruth H. Chung point out that "English-speaking Korean Americans have forged their own religiosity that borrows from the immigrant congregations that have been part of their upbringing, but also from campus ministries, pan-Asian, and multi-racial/ethnic religious settings."[38] Improvisation within Asian American religious practices are really about "the adaptability, flexibility, and continuing innovation of individuals, institutions, and communities as they live out and practice their religion and spirituality."[39] These emergent expressions of faith are created not merely to satisfy particular needs of people at a given time but speak of some deeper significance. The Buddhist-Christian funeral service following the tragic incident at Cleveland School and Keut Chun's creation of the morning ritual are not just a convenient compromise for the Southeast Asian American communities in Stockton, California. They are indicative of the communities' actual practice of faith and the interpenetration of divergent cosmological orientations in their lives. For one thing, these new and amphibolous practices of faith stem from the value orientation of harmony and an affirmation of the web of life rather than a boundary-making and an oppositional dynamic of relationship that is prevalent in the American society and culture. This non-oppositional religious sensitivity is behind the tolerance and acceptance of familiar religious traditions and the absence of contradictory dualism. Embodied cosmologies and worldviews, or "tonalities" of life accounts expressed in various faith traditions often co-mingle with each other in the religious practices of Asian Americans. A positional superiority is not necessarily accorded to any one particular faith tradition. In such an amphibolous setting the *apriori* character of

---

37. Niebuhr, *Radical Monotheism and Western Culture*.
38. Yoo and Chung, *Religion and Spirituality in Korean America*, 15.
39. Ibid., 16.

Christ's revelatory event in Christianity is contained within the mutually co-existing faith traditions of Asia, thereby making Christianity's monotheistic cosmology non-normative.

Another example of resistance against the forces of interpellation is found in the Japanese and Japanese American concentration campus during World War II. Historian Gary Okihiro examines the Buddhist-Christian complexities in the resistance to the religion of missionaries. Religious symbols and stories are appropriated and Asians/Asian Americans make Christianity their own.[40] The interpenetration of religious traditions and cosmologies in the practice of faith for Asian Americans is in large part based on the formation of our own communities and our affirmation of our own subjectivities. Conventionally understood, Christians believe that a common belief brings people together. But Yen Le Espiritu reminds us that an imposed identity may also offer an opportunity to create a community's own distinct coherence, or "panethnicity."[41] No longer separated by old world political conflicts, languages, and customs, Asian Americans see the political necessity and social advantages of uniting and speaking with one voice in the U.S. At the same time, panethnicity is not solely an imposed identity. It is "a political resource for insiders, a basis on which to mobilize diverse peoples and to force others to be more responsive to their grievances and agendas."[42] Cosmology arises out of the similarities of identities forged in the process of this new identity making. In this sense, cosmology is an expression of an emerging group culture that is simultaneously a boundary marker and a product of boundary. "Because panethnic groups are new groups, any real or perceived cultural commonality cannot lay claim to a primordial origin. Instead, panethnic unity is forged primarily through the symbolic reinterpretation of a group's common history, particularly when this history involves racial subjugation."[43] The production of a new cosmological orientation for Asian Americans is thus tied to the panethnic identity and community formation that is currently underway. The panethnic identity is yet another amphibolous expression of Asian American lives.

---

40. Okihiro, "Religion and Resistance in America's Concentration Camps."
41. Espiritu, *Asian American Women and Men*.
42. Ibid., 7.
43. Ibid., 9.

More often than not, amphibolous faith is expressed as an acknowledgment, perhaps even a resignation or acceptance, of irreconcilable differences that co-exist within a person or a community that do not call for a resolution or an easy reconciliation of differences. For Asian American Christians in particular, faith is likely to be expressed as a domain of myriad conflicting faith traditions coming together in a person. Dis-identification with a singular faith tradition, or non-compartmentalization of faiths, is as much material as religious in nature. It is the material side of life that often informs a non-singular faith orientation deeply rooted in Asian Americans even amidst the powerful interpellative forces raining upon us. Lisa Lowe theorizes the interpellative societal context in which the dis-identification with a particular faith tradition is located, focusing on what she calls "Immigrant acts," the *contradictions* of Asian immigration, placing Asian Americans "'within' the U.S. nation-state, its workplaces, and its markets, yet linguistically, culturally, and racially marked [them] as 'foreign' and 'outside' the national policy."[44]

"I guess I'm part-Buddhist, part-Christian and part nothing at all," says Kiku.[45] Amphibolous faith is aporetic in that it is the experience of the "undecidable," a domain that especially becomes acute for Asian American Christians who are assumed or expected to embrace the monotheistic claims of the historically inherited Christian faith as it is expressed through the medium of metaphysics. And yet, among Asian Americans are those who are inclined to live with non-theistic cosmologies embedded in Asian religious traditions that are more ontological in epistemology than metaphysical. A person of amphibolous faith thus creates one's own grammar that defies a conventional articulation. Indeed, such a person is a "disorienting subject" who "refuse to be subsumed under the dominant methods and approaches of either Religious or Asian American studies as they have developed."[46] This is so because it is likely for a person of amphibolous faith to acknowledge the constellation of relationships among various material dimensions of faith associated with life. A person of amphibolous faith not only defies conventional faith paradigms but also lives in an asymmetrical domain, caught among whatever is the dominant paradigm and, at the

---

44. Lowe, *Immigrant Acts*, 9.
45. Uchida, *Picture Bride*, 13.
46. Busto, "Disorienting Subjects," 24.

same time, multiple other faith traditions often ignored and devalued and yet still very much alive in oneself or in one's community. In this sense, amphibolous faith is truly "hybrid," a term that points not to a free oscillation between or among chosen religious identities, but to an uneven process through which immigrant communities encounter various expressions of violence in America. It is the process through which we survive the violence by living, inventing, and reproducing different cultural and faith alternatives. Amphibolous faith is also a life posture with a heightened sense of the poignancy of the materially shadow side of life. This is so because the awareness of an *aporia*, a fissure, among various cosmologies, worldviews, and faith traditions, is an awareness of asymmetrical relationships.

In other words, an amphibolous faith is often expressed by those Asian American Christians who inhabit the translocal existence of "not quite being at home in one's home." This amphibolous experience of homelessness largely derives from a spirit of dissonance, dissent or discordance with the prevailing civil religion in U.S. society. More specifically, the source of this amphibolous deracination is located within the fissure between the powerful interpellative Abrahamic faiths and the Asian cosmological and faith orientations that are transported into a new land and are transformed into embodied experiences of a translocal people both religiously and materially. The sensibility expressed by the term "amphiboly" is not a privilege but rather a marginalizing alternative to the traditionally prevalent readings of Christianity. It is a discontinuous state of faith, a solitude experienced as a breaking away from a dominating group in order to remain faithful to one's multiplicity. Furthermore, this fissuring is driven by an urgent need to reconstitute and rehabilitate broken lives, usually by those who see themselves living with the dominant ideology but whose existence is on the fringe.

Unfortunately, the discordant sense of homelessness we have been discussing is not exclusive to the experience of Asian American Christians. Regardless of cultural or religious appellation, those in the U.S. whose faith is amphibolous are forced to accept the necessity of living within the interpellative dominant ideology and material conditions, while at the same time being driven by the desire to reassemble their broken history into a new whole. Nevertheless, people for whom faith is amphibolous are aware that such a restoration and rehabilitation is likely to be unattainable given the histories of failed attempts to establish a restored community in such groups as Native Americans, Palestinians, as well as Asian Americans ourselves. Thus, an amphibolous faith exists in the precarious state of lacking any assurance of a glorious future. But those who embrace amphibolous faith still *provisionally* insist on and believe in "planting an apple tree even if the world comes to its end tomorrow." In amphibolous faith there is a *cantus firmus,* a firm and clear tone, well crafted, so that the contrapuntal parts of the melody of life can be respected. The pathos of amphibolous faith indelibly etches its mark on the life of Asian American Christians' faith.

Amphibolous faith suggests that the alternative to an exclusive belief is not simply unbelief but a different kind of belief, one that embraces irresoluteness, disruption, even uncertainty, and enables the believer to respect that which we do not understand. In a complex world, wisdom is the knowledge that one does not really know for certain. This wisdom directs the amphibolous believer to keep the future open, with a provisional stance of faith as the only guide. The person of amphibolous faith longs, most of all, for a bridge-building amidst disrupted and estranged relationships, a bridge-building whose real meaning is an interpretation of the worlds through the grammar of amphiboly.

The production of an amphibolous faith is at the level where the present state of the epistemological distinctness of Asian American faith practices can be observed. Moreover, the emergence of the hybridized cosmology and faith practices corresponds to the construction of a collective identity and the subjectivity claim of Asian Americans amidst the material context of race, gender, sexuality and translocal existence in this society. In much of the social science and religious literature in the U.S., this dimension of faith understanding has been neglected.

The North Atlantic constellations of the normativity of radical monotheism have often been taken for granted in analyzing the emerging religious expressions in the current circle of theological discussions. H. Richard Niebuhr explores the question of "radical monotheism" from the standpoint of human faith understood not as belief but as trust in and loyalty to active powers or realities that "make life worth living."[47]

---

47. The description of God or the gods as realities that "make life worth living" appears repeatedly in Niebuhr's writing. See, for example, *The Meaning of Revelation,* 77; and *Radical Monotheism and Western Culture,* 116 ff.. Tolstoy's *My Confession* to which Niebuhr refers in *Radical Monotheism and Western Culture,* 18–21, and Santayana's concept of "animal faith" as referred to in *Scepticism And Animal Faith* are among the sources of the description, though it was doubtless rooted in personal experience: see

From this point of view, there are many such realities and powers and therefore many deities in human history. They range from relatively inclusive realms of being and action such as nature or humanity or life to exclusive powers such as nations, religions and churches, the home or the self. They may even be abstract values such as truth or justice that even though abstract exercise power over us. No one lives without trust in and loyalty to one or more such realities. There are no unbelievers from the standpoint of this understanding of faith and the gods or the God of faith. "Atheism in this sense is no more a live alternative for us in our actual personal existence than psychological solipsism is in our physical life. To deny the reality of a supernatural being called God is one thing; to live without confidence in some center of value, without loyalty to a cause is another."[48]

Niebuhr's identifies three forms of human faith in his analysis of those centers of value and objects of loyalty to which people of Western culture have been oriented in their long history. One is henotheism, a confidence in and loyalty to a single limited and finite power, albeit one god among many. The second is a contemporary version of polytheism, a diffused and conflicted trust in and loyalty to several finite centers of value and objects of loyalty. The third is a form of faith oriented to infinite reality and power, inclusive of the finite, to which human faith on rare occasions has turned in trust and loyalty. Following both Hebrew and the Greek traditions, Niebuhr calls this reality the "One," and Niebuhr gives the name "radical monotheism" to the form of human faith oriented to the One. It is a form of faith rarely if ever found in a pure form either within or outside of religious communities, including the Christian church. It has appeared "more as hope than as datum,"

"Reformation; Continuing Imperative." In Niebuhr's view the self has no existence apart from its relations and attempts by the self to make itself the center of value and object of loyalty are an illusion. In the main text of *Radical Monotheism and Western Culture* Niebuhr writes of Epicureanism and Existentialism as efforts by "the most critical and most self-conscious men" to center faith as trust and loyalty around "isolated selfhood." Epicureanism fails in this effort because it actually finds "its center . . . in something imposed on the self, the pain-and-pleasure feeling that is the constant accompaniment of conscious existence." Existentialism is "a more robust assertion of faith seeking a center in the self and a cause projected by a self." But in fact it is not so much a faith "in the self but of a self, and it is confidence in nothing; its cause is not the self but the self projecting itself toward nothing" (28–29). Niebuhr, *Radical Monotheism Western Culture*, 24–25.

48. Niebuhr, *Radical Monotheism and Western Culture*, 15.

more as a "qualification" of other forms of faith than a fully emergent reality. It is known only "in passing moments and the clarified intervals of personal existence." In this sense, cosmologies have always been closely interwoven with the structural elements of a society that have been central in their development. All the more the reason one needs to acknowledge, the interpellative forces are at work in the American society.

For Asian Americans, the correspondence between an embodied cosmology and identity construction is due primarily to our marginalized social and cultural status. A close correlation between the religious and cosmological dimensions of life and the claim for subjectivity in the material culture of race, class, gender, sexuality, and translocal life is of crucial importance in shaping the dynamics of Asian American communities and of the pattern of their social order. In examining such relationships, there emerge a few discernable issues regarding cosmological tonalities and their relation to faith practices. Amphibolous faith expressions depend upon the trust of Asian Americans in an epistemology that reflects their particular life experiences; to wit, "reality" is multiple. This amphibolous faith, and the epistemology that supports it, contravenes the familiar American epistemological and "grammatological" constructions of "one in many." Reality is indeed multiple. This is the bottom-line trust that undergirds an amphibolous faith. Unlike henotheism or polytheism, amphiboly is predicated upon an implicit trust in multiple expressions of community-building, a sense of belonging to each other, and a web of relationships that connects the entire community. This is the epistemological foundation of amphiboly.

THE EPISTEMOLOGY OF AN AMPHIBOLOUS FAITH: THE COURAGE TO IMAGINE LIFE AS OTHERS LIVE IT

What then is the epistemological history and significance of amphiboly in the history of Asian American religious discourse? It can be said that certitude is not a valued faith expression in the discourse. Uncertainties, ambivalences, and ambiguities of Asian American life experiences are often highlighted. One could ask, even in Asian American Christian communities, whether there may be certain areas of faith practices where inherited theological knowledge from the West is expected to be more "resistant" and less "relative" than created interpretations. The traditioning process, *actus tradendi, of* Christian faith therefore takes an increasingly complex shape as these questions and issues around amphibolous faith are examined.

Martin Buber's term, "Holy Insecurity," was utilized quite profitably by a group of Asian American religious educators in order to describe the practices of Christian faith in Asian American communities.[49]

> We look for security in this life but seldom find it. We are driven to look for meaning regarding our own situation. If we don't find meaning in our present condition, we look for an alternative which has promise of short term satisfaction. Once we begin to look to this relationship to the Ultimate Power, we discover tremendous possibilities open to us. We are introduced to real freedom.[50]

What makes this use of "Holy Insecurity" so profound is its early theological expression set within the racialized and translocal existence of Asian American Christians coupled with the inherited Asian cosmological views recognized by the religious educators in 1970s. The sensibility expressed by the term "Holy Insecurity" arose out of a discontinuous state of being, a solitude experienced outside a dominating group by Asian Americans in the tumultuous eras of the 1960s and 70s, when the identity consciousness of Asian Americans began to emerge. The crucial thing is that those whose faith is "Holy Insecurity" desired to be free from the dominant ideology and was driven by the desire to reassemble their new identities. Since the early 1970s, when the study of religion among Asian Americans matured with the introduction of "Holy Insecurity," there has been an influx of new immigrants and their families from Asia into the U.S. An explosion of immigrant churches, temples, and other religious organizations accompanied a boom in the Asian American population. Correspondingly, the religious sensibilities of Asian Americans have evolved into various distinct expressions of rituals and practices with a heightened consciousness of race and translocality. However, over time it became apparent among Asian American leaders that the term "Holy Insecurity" as coined by Buber did not adequately connote the power imbalance that is inherent in the relationship between Asian Americans and the dominant racial groups of North

---

49. *Sojourners in Asian-American and Biblical History*, 37f.
50. Ibid.

Atlantic origin. Terms that have emerged in Asian American discourse in last two decades—such as "liminality," "interstitiality," and "marginality"—more accurately express the reality of Asian Americans' religious practices than the term "Holy Insecurity."

As reflected in numerous publications of Asian American literature, these more recent terms, sometimes borrowed from anthropology, are,may be expressive of silence: imposed silence, the silence of meaning, the silence of the Divine. The novel *Obasan*, by the Japanese-Canadian writer Kogawa, is one of the representative works on the theme of silence. It is a story of the mass relocation of West Coast Japanese Canadians during World War II.[51] The story begins with Naomi, the narrator, visiting her aunt Obasan following the death of her Uncle. On the kitchen counter Naomi sees a hard, black loaf of bread made by Uncle before his death. This "stone bread" serves as a powerful symbol that repeatedly appears throughout the novel, either as a material object or in figures of speech. The "stone bread" motif is multifaceted in meaning. It speaks of the hardships, deprivations, and dislocations suffered by Japanese Canadians during the war. It also represents a mystery and silence surrounding Naomi's mother, who visited Nagasaki and died at the time of the atomic bombing. Her disfiguring and subsequent death was withheld from Naomi and her brother. Juxtaposed with the dual Christian symbols of bread and stone, Kogawa introduces the Eucharistic significance of the bread coupled with the role Naomi's mother plays in her life. The story can be read through a conventional notion of God's redemptive grace given to Naomi in her personal life, and also within the context of the Japanese-Canadian community. Upon closer reading and observation, however, the central significance of the "stone bread" motif suggests something else. After Naomi learns about what happened to her mother in Nagasaki from Sensei, a Christian pastor, the following scene ensues:

> Stephen (Naomi's brother) is staring at the floor . . . I sit on a stool beside him and try to concentrate on what is being said. I can hear Aunt Emily telling us about Mother's grave. Then Nakayama-sensei stands and begins to say the Lord's Prayer under his breath . . . he repeats, sighing deeply, "as we forgive others . . ." He lifts his head, looking upwards. "We are powerless to forgive unless we first are forgiven. It is a high calling my friends—the calling to

---

51. Kogawa, *Obasan*.

> forgive. But no person, no people is innocent. Therefore we must forgive one another."
>
> I am not thinking of forgiveness. The sound of Sensei's voice grows as indistinct as the hum of distant traffic. Gradually the room grows still and it is as if I am back with Uncle again, listening and listening to the silent earth and the silent sky as I have done all my life.
> I close my eyes.
> Mother. I am listening. Assist me to hear you.[52]

The meaning of the Eucharist is here transformed by an overarching cosmology of belonging and longing that is rooted more in the Asian religious traditions rather than in the Abrahamic faith traditions. The Japanese notion of *amae*—unconditional mutual dependence, expressed largely within a hierarchical relationship such as a parent and child—whose root is in Jodo Shinshu Buddhism, is the underpinning of Emily's faith. "I am not thinking of forgiveness.... Mother. I am listening. Assist me to hear you," says Emily.

> There is a silence that cannot speak. There is a silence that will not speak. Beneath the grass the speaking dreams and beneath the dreams is a sensate sea. The speech that frees comes forth from the amniotic deep. To attend its voice, I can hear it say, is to embrace its silence. But I fail the task. The word is stone.[53]

In this narration and in other writings by Asian American writers, faith is depicted not in a monotheistic, rational, and exclusive fashion. It is encompassing of different Asian religious traditions and practices without resorting to a doctrinal resolution of incommensurability, one from another. Moreover, faith is so down to earth, mundane and polymorphic that it melts into the fabric of life without occupying a separate and distinct dimension in one's existence. It neither divides the world into either/or nor into separate realms of sacred and secular. Such a posture is also echoed in Nellie Wong's "Day of the Dead": "if I worship the dead, it is because I hear my parents whispering through the marrow of my bones asking to be fed."[54]

---

52. Ibid., 240.
53. Ibid., iii.
54. Wong, *Dreams in Harrison Railroad Park*, 120.

The absence of a conflictual dualism is not an inherited legacy of an Asian past. It is a refusal on the part of Asian American writers to accept the myths that have prevented their past from being fully accessible to the present generation. Contemporary Asian American writers are often forced to try to piece together and sort out the meaning of the past from shreds of stories heard in childhood or from faded photographs that have never been fully explained by their parents and grandparents. In this sense, the non-conflictual dualistic posture of life is subversively political as well as cosmological. In other words, such a non-oppositional dualistic posture of Asian Americans politically challenges a religious and social system that privileges belief over practice, ideology over behavior, exclusive allegiance over generous hospitality.

To label such a reality as intellectually unsophisticated in the study of faiths is to miss the significance of the profound shift that is taking place, first among the Asian American population but also in the wider society as well. This emerging spiritual trajectory is not a nostalgic return to the old Asian spirituality. It is, rather, an imaginative posture about the directions in which we might be moving. It recognizes that the future will reward those who anticipate the institutions and procedures we shall need based on the cosmologies and worldviews that we are beginning to trust. For Asian American writers such as Maxine Hong Kingston, Yoshiko Uchida, and Joy Kogawa, faith is deeply mundane, egalitarian, practical, and communal. It is rooted in the fragile and often disenfranchised religious traditions of Asia that are mutilated but still tenaciously kept alive in the new setting of North America as "cultural DNA." The emergence of this new expression of faith is imaginatively creative and adaptive, all the while *within* an equally tenacious and hostile setting dominated by an outmoded and corrupt cosmology that privileges ideological certainty, rationalistic elitism, and exclusivism. In the words of Rita Nakashima Brock,

> [W]e must retrieve, reexamine, and reconstruct our various Asian American religious identities.... Connecting with the ancestors (read: history, suffering, imagination, struggle, texts, ritual) is the place to begin.... texts must be approached with a hermeneutic of suspicion. A dialogic approach to texts, where reader and text lead to what Gadamer calls "fusion of horizons" may, in fact, idealize both the tradition and the interpreter. We cannot afford to fetishize what we *think* is the original tradition or "authorized" interpretation/translation, or privilege one indi-

vidual's reading over another's without understanding the range of possible readings of a text. It is the possibility of readings along a continuum of subject positions and quests that, for example, allows the Bhagavad Gita to authorize the contrasting spiritual *margas* (paths) of devotion, duty, and unattachment.

Neither must we fall into the error of limiting our work through the compartmentalization or protection of our "home" cultures as pristine or static. Recall that Islam, Buddhism and Roman Catholicism all moved swiftly throughout Asia taking on the characteristic of local peoples. Neither should we be afraid of religious symbiosis in the revitalization of Asian American religious identities.

Asian Americans, in their multiplicity of parent traditions and locations in the United States must take the initiative and responsibility for producing our own sutras, analyses of self, sacred languages, and placating our particular Gold Mountain ancestors . . . As scholars concerned not only with the sal-vaging of Asian American religious histories, but also with responsible constructive work for Asian American communities, it is imperative that we frame our analyses in conjunction with the very communities that determine and define Asian American religious identities.[55]

The responsible constructive work for Asian American faith communities is thus undertaken amidst the material construction of community identitiy *with* the notions of race, gender, translocal life, sexuality and class. Gramasci's notion of hegemony applies here as well, as not the political rule but also a process within which any specific dominant configuration exists, always within the context of contesting pressures from other sites, classes, and groups in different conditions of self-identification and formation. The trivialization of the class, gender, and race contradiction in the construction of American national identity is precisely the ground from which newly emerging cosmological and epistemological orientations becomes possible.

In a society increasingly preoccupied with a truncated expression of the first tongue of American democracy, the sense of entitlement as expressed in "free-market fundamentalism, aggressive militarism, and escalating authoritarianism," what is needed in reclaiming a societal coherence, that is, *peoplehood*, is nurturing another tongue, a second tongue, in order to have the courage to imagine life as others live it. We need a second tongue in order to "*change* [our] *perspective on how* [we]

---

55. Brock, "Response-Clearing," 189–90.

build [our] interests and how [we] defend them by building a network of relationships that take into consideration the interests of others who are weak and who have rights but are incapable of imposing these interests or these rights."[56]

In our increasingly diverse population, not only in terms of race, culture, and religion, but equally in terms of wealth, class, and power, we need the capacity to see life contrapuntally. "*With the lives of the diverse characters starkly juxtaposed—in constant counterpoint . . . creates a world that offers both biting criticism and profound sympathy*" at the same time, says Said.[57] Such a contrapuntal task for the renewal of peoplehood seeks a mutual consideration of otherwise incongruent social, economic, and political practices, culture and history, with particular attention given to the practices, cultures, histories and faiths that have been neglected and undervalued. Amphibolous faith, with its own epistemological view of the world, provides a glimpse of such a counter-perspective of our collective life. A new peoplehood may have a chance to be born in a world in which a second tongue is readily spoken, a second tongue that welcomes an amphibolous faith. In the world of this second tongue, eluding certainty will be prized as a value that propels us into action, especially in those contexts where the exploitation of those who are at the underside of life is palpable. From this responsible reaction to the diminishment of our fellow human beings, it is not difficult to perceive that amphiboly has its necessary place. What is now required is the commitment to allow our imaginations to work on transforming our minds and hearts, informing our lips and hands, inspiring our thoughts and actions so that our amphibolous faith is recognized and valued for what it offers—that when we think we have grasped reality, whatever our intentions be, the reality passes through our minds, in front of us, eludes us, and goes on its way.

---

56. Semaan, quoted in Wall, "Eyes to See," 45.
57. Said, "Huxley's Point Counter Point."

Conclusion

ELUDING CERTAINTY: THE COURAGE TO IMAGINE LIFE AS OTHERS LIVE IT

THIS STORY IS ABOUT a re-discovery of the proper role of democracy in today's America, a re-discovery that is made by an excavation into a "second language" that has been indispensible for the story of our nation and what the nation stands for. In mid-nineteenth century Alexis de Tocqueville identified possible threats to the republican representative form of democracy in America.[1] Tocqueville pointed out that the threats and dangers to American democracy include a possibility of the nation degenerating into "soft despotism" and a tyranny of the majority. Cornell West in our days rephrases the threats and dangers facing democracy as: "free-market fundamentalism," "aggressive militarism" and "escalating authoritarianism."[2] These threats and dangers to democracy exist in the midst of an increasing awareness by Americans about the diverse character of our society in a globalized world. As Herman Melville said over one hundred years ago, America has been settled by "the people of all nations . . . . You can not spill a drop of American blood, without spilling the blood of the whole world."[3] We are "not a narrow tribe."[4] The varied voices of the "people of all nations," orchestrated side-by-side together, tell the complicated but hopeful story of America

1. Tocqueville, *Democracy in America*, 425.
2. West, *Democracy Matters*.
3. Melville, *Moby Dick* quoted by Ron Takaki, *Different Mirror*.
4. Ibid.

as a nation peopled by the world. The story of America is an unfolding one. The nation was founded and "dedicated," to use Lincoln's language in the Gettysburg Address, "to equality as a "self-evident truth." But this very principle of equality, as Lincoln also noted, has been a proposition. To make it a reality remains the unfinished work of Americans. In order to fully understand this self-evident truth about the diverse character of America in which the republican and representative form of democracy functions, we need a "different mirror" as historian Ronald Takaki puts it.[5] The epic story of America is told not only from the top-down, the perspectives of the rich and powerful, but, more importantly, from the bottom-up, through the lives, experiences, and stories of everyday people, that is, the stories told in second tongue, the languages spoken by those Americans whose voices often counter the vocal and powerful elites. Their varied voices spoken in second tongue, orchestrated side-by-side together, tell the complicated but hopeful story of America and its peoplehood.

And yet, today at this critical moment in American history with its nervousness about the very character of America, diversity explodes across our society and as policymakers seek to criminalize and incarcerate undocumented immigrants. The romanticized notion of America's racial and ethnic mix inspiring idealism of melting pot is contrary of the disturbing reality of our society today. The enhanced awareness of diversity in America tend to cause those who actually live with neighbors, co-workers, fellow students of different racial, ethnic, and life-style backgrounds to withdraw and retreat into their own shells, producing what political scientist Robert Putnam a "turtle effect." "Diversity, at least in the short run, seems to bring out the turtle in all of us," he says.[6] What is disturbing in Putnam's findings is that the greater the diversity in an area, the less trust Americans have in neighbors and the more isolated we become one from another. That lack of trust and the erosion of a societal coherence show up in a variety of ways; the people are less likely to register to vote, do less volunteering, give less to charity, have fewer close friends, and are less happy. While Putnam is somewhat optimistic about America's future, the challenges facing us to cope with the enhanced awareness of our national diversity remains. "Over time, especially with some thought and care, we

5. Takaki, *Different Mirror.*
6. Putnam, quoted in the *Christian Science Monitor.*

can get used to diversity," Putnam says. "That's what the country has done in the past, and that's what the country is going through now."[7] But diversity is not always necessarily a "good thing" just as it has a potential to be a good thing. It could derail the societal coherence of peoplehood by the nation to degenerate into "soft despotism" and a tyranny of the majority, or "free-market fundamentalism," "aggressive militarism" and "escalating authoritarianism" even in the name of democracy. In the international arena, our nation of diversity could invite a new form of isolationism even in the globalized era.

The message of this book is that democracy should not be essentialized as a universal sacred cow for America. It has its own historical and cultural context from which it originated. Once we realize the historically contingent and contexual nature of democracy, then we should be able to critique its limits. That is what George Semaan was attempting to do. That is to say that democracy needs to be tempered by the relational nature of human life that takes into consideration the voices of those who have rights but who are unable to exercise the rights. In today's increasingly polarizing world politically, religiously, economically and militarily, we need to pay a close attention more than ever before to the significance of the web of humanity and its accompanying implications and challenges. In addition to the warnings voiced by Tocqueville and West about the threats and dangers of American form of democracy, we are today also faced with other forms of threats and dangers. One is our democracy becoming "upward mobility." Richard Neuhaus describes this danger:

> . . . late Christopher Lasch depicted the unhappy circumstance of our last several decades as a 'betrayal of the elites.' The elites, he said, have come to define democracy not in terms of self-governance but of upward mobility. '[The overlcass] is marked by an overbearing quality; it presents itself as being over and against the American people but is quite unable to give any good reasons for its pretensions to superiority. The encouraging thing is that an overclass cannot sustain itself as a ruling class because it offers no argument for its right to rule.'"[8]

The widening economic gap between the super-rich and the rest of the American populace already confirms this disturbing equation of de-

---

7. Ibid.
8 Neuhaus, "Farewell to the Overclass," 64–80.

mocracy with economic and social upward mobility. Another area of the essentialized expression of democracy is the place of American culture in the age of global capitalism. The positive side of American culture is its remarkable openness to enrichment from other cultures despite the danger of its economic exploitation and political and military domination. American culture has managed to be open to the gifts of the many peoples and cultures of the world. One powerful instrument of this openness is English language. Our common language of English is mediated through American culture but in a deeper sense it is a global creation, perhaps the first truly global language. The negative side of American English language is its powerful techno-scientific commitment to autonomous definitions of freedom and progress. This commitment "may also be destroying the ecological, social, and religious foundations of the life system on planet earth. Modern American freedom and progress may be producing their dialectical opposites. American culture seems to be propagandizing the world with a trivialized definition of sexuality and massive celebration of violence."[9] Philosopher of religion Joe Holland says:

> As globalization proceeds at an increasingly faster pace, the individualistic and consumeristic aspects of modern American culture are gaining the upper hand in the global traffic of information, ideas, and values . . . The emphasis on sex and violence, the exclusively individualistic focus, the consumerist ethos, ultimate criterion of money, and commodification of life itself are corruption. Even the Wall Street financier George Soros has called attention to the threat that the values propagated by global laissez-faire capitalism poses to the very values on which open and democratic societies depend.[10]

Under the American form of democracy the character of individualism has changed. The traditional style, echoing Franklin and Emerson, turned on self-reliance, achievement what sociologists call utilitarian individualism. But a newer style of individualism has blossomed in recent decades. It is expressive individualism. It is about emotional gratification, self-help, getting in touch with feelings, expressing personal needs. Utilitarian individualism is the ideology of "going West" as expressed in the Manifest Destiny whereas expressive individualism

---

9. Holland, "Faith and Culture."
10. Holland, "The Capitalist Threat," 45–58.

is going to the forest, on Robert Bly's advice, to find your inner essence. "What aspect of your life is most fulfilling or satisfying, 'more than half mention family, children or marriage' far more than any other aspect of life. And yet most people (77 percent) agreed that 'because of such things as divorce, more working mothers, single parents, etc., family ties in the U.S. are breaking down.'"[11] Americans also view religion in expressively an individualistic way. Historically 'being religious' implies actively participating in worship, fellowship and other aspects or organized religious life. Most Americans do not think religious participation is as important as one's faith and moral code. Andrew J. Cherlin speaks for the current notion of religion for Americans. "Religion to me means belonging to a specific congregation or denomination, and that is no longer very important today." Today "faith means something I found myself, not something I learned in grade school or something someone told me I had. It's very much a personal thing."[12] This wariness of organized religion and lack of interpersonal trust could be taken as evidence of a broader change in Americans' sense of self: declining involvement in civic groups, neighborhoods and communities. Alex de Tocqueville thought that American democracy worked, in part, because of the many local citizens' groups that could influence government and counter its power. Americans are forming "loose connections" that can compensate somewhat for the decline in other forms of civic life.

Americans like to lament their individualistic bent, all the while pursuing it. They also care about commitments to others, all the while changing partners, jobs and neighborhoods. Both sentiments "individualism and commitment" are genuine. But the most fundamental quality of the American sense of self is neither individualism nor commitment but rather our continuing ambivalence as we steer a life course between them. The higher living standard of advanced capitalism has reduced the need for support from others and thus for strong lifetime commitments. It has allowed more Americans to steer toward expressive individualism. They relish the levels of personal achievement and emotional gratification that they have attained as a result. But as is clear from their complaints about others and their anxieties about themselves, they're beginning to recognize the price.

11. Cherlin, "Am O.k., You're Selfish," 44f.
12. Ibid.

This is to say that individualism profoundly impacts American democracy. John A. Coleman as with Bellah noted that even secular analysts acknowledge that the preponderance of citizen action in this country is rooted in communities of religious faith. He sharply criticizes theorists such as ethicist John Rawls who contend that religious discourse can have no legitimate place in public debate. John A. Coleman renders an important service by reminding us of the enduring power of the bigotries that would exclude religion from public discourse, and by lifting up once again the importance of voluntarism and mediating institutions to the vitality of American democracy.[13] The role of religious faith in its shaping of American democracy is further complicated by the religious diversity in recent years. A degree of incomprehension is the price minorities pay for the blessings of tolerance. The reluctance of Americans to confront the root of religious beliefs and practices in their midst—the "live-and-let-live approach"—is an expression not of Christian triumphalism but of longstanding civic norms. We tiptoe around one another's faiths because, publicly anyway, Americans aren't supposed to be accountable for what conscience demands of them. In the United States, a certain amount of incomprehension in society at large is the reasonable price that religious minorities—Roman Catholics and Jews no less than today's Muslims, Buddhists and Hindus—have always paid for the blessings of tolerance.[14]

What is needed in today's world is the recognition that one's own conviction, faith, piety, and worldview are not an end-all. We need to recognize that there is "more" to life than what we each individually and communally know and embrace. This sense of "more" is often expressed religiously and transcendentally but also in the human sphere as Charles Taylor argues.[15] Religion is not a projection of human mind as Nietzsche argued but that we human beings are indeed an extension of what we believe and trust the "more" to be. In other words, what we believe is not the ultimate. We need the sense of openness and receptiveness to something beyond our own individual values and convictions. What we need today is a recovery of the relational nature of human and ecological

---

13. See Neuhaus, *Naked Public Square*.
14. Wuthnow, *Religious Diversity*.
15. Taylor, *A Secular Age*.

life where the values such as caring of others, integrity of the self, and trust in the openness of the future are nurtured.[16]

We have argued in this work that the epistemological basis from which such task of reclaiming the basic relational nature of life lies, particularly in America, the recovery of the second languages that have nurtured our peoplehood. The recovery of second languages is based on what Rudy Busto articulated in his early work on "disorienting subjects."[17] What is "disorienting" for Americans is the need to reexamine the take-for-granted foundation of our nation, that is, democratic freedom. Karen Hughes' comment before Congress about America being involved in a generational and global struggle of ideas of spreading democracy and freedom throughout the world is not the real challenge facing America's peoplehood.[18] David Rieff's question about Hughes' comment indeed reveals the limits of the current exercise of democracy. "Refreshing though it was for its candor, Hughes' statement neglected the larger question: Is hostility toward the United States based largely on misperceptions of America's actions and intentions or on a genuine dislike of the power America wields around the world?"[19] In order to believe that the traditional American ideals should prevail if only these ideals are communicated well enough, then " . . . you must believe that there is an inevitable progress in history—a progress toward freedom."[20] This basic assumption about an inevitable progress in history is behind the current U.S. foreign policies. This question is becoming increasingly questionable in today's world both within the U.S. and abroad. The view that the role of the U.S. in the world is to spread its understanding of democratic freedom and of the belief in the global application of the progress toward freedom is indeed deeply ingrained in the American psyche from the foundation of this nation's history. This belief has been reinforced particularly in the time of wars. Democratic freedom is the foundation of our society, rooted in our collective history and continues to be affirmed and reaffirmed in every critical turn of events in our nation. It is what gives rise to the questions that frame my current work:

16. I owe this insight to theologian Warren Groff and his book *Christ the Hope of the Future: Signals of Promised Humanity.*
17. Busto, "Disorienting Self."
18. Rieff, "Their Hearts And Minds?" 11.
19. Ibid.
20. Ibid.

- Is it democratic freedom that is still the dominant source today for the cultivating of societal coherence for Americans and for our relationship with our world neighbors?
- Will our current understanding of democratic freedom contribute to global peace and justice in a world suspicious and hostile toward U.S. and the way it wields its power?
- Or, in order to embody the relational character of peoplehood, does America need to reexamine its own democratic principles and values so as to temper these principles and values in such a way that takes into consideration the well-being of our neighbors at home and abroad?

The answers we give to these questions have specific implications for the state of American democracy with its distinct Christian origin. Bellah and his colleagues have argued that one of the keys to the survival of democratic free institutions is the "relationship between private and public life, the way in which citizens do, or do not, participate in the public sphere."[21] But the question still persists: What motivates American people to participate in the public sphere? In our increasingly plural society these traditions and numerous second languages are not limited to be based on the republican and biblical traditions. America needs to recover and value the numerous second languages that have been spoken but often neglected and devalued in this land, the languages that help America recognize the critical challenge of the recovery of peoplehood in the future. More than ever before America needs the recovery of its second languages in order to participate in the wider public sphere. George Semaan's words are prophetic in today's America. America needs to "change its perspective on how it builds its interests and how it defends them by building a network of relationships that takes into consideration the interests of others who are weak and who have rights but are incapable of imposing these interests or these rights."[22] Such a task is indeed disorienting precisely because it challenges the basic assumptive values that lie in our society. And yet, the task needs not start from a blank sheet. The seeds for the reexamination of democratic principles and values lie in the languages, the second languages, spoken by the very "disorienting subjects," have already begun

21. Bellah, *Habits of the Heart*, viii.
22. Semaan, quoted in Wall, "Eyes to See," 45.

in certain corners of our land such as in Asian American communities in their articulation of the epistemological foundations.

A CONTRAPUNTAL TASK FOR THE RENEWAL OF PEOPLEHOOD

In our increasingly diverse population, not only in terms of race, culture, sexuality, and religion, but, equally in terms of wealth, class, and power, we need a capacity to see life contrapuntally. "With the lives of the diverse characters starkly juxtaposed—in constant counterpoint . . . [to create] a world that offers both biting criticism and profound sympathy" at the same time, says Edward Said.[23] Such a contrapuntal task for the renewal of peoplehood seeks mutual consideration of otherwise incongruent social, economic, and political practices, of culture, of history with particular attention given to the practices, cultures, histories, and faiths that have been neglected and undervalued. The amphibolous faith with its own epistemological view of the world provides a glimpse of such a counter-perspective of our collective life. This view begins with the notion that reality is multiple. The depth-reality is not one but many. People with amphibolous faith live with *aparia*, "undecidable," a refusal to be acquiesced into a singular vision precisely because of such a people's experiences of the contradiction inherent in their beings of both the "foreigner within" and "model minority." The crucial point to understand is that those whose faith is amphibolous are accepting the necessity to live with the pressure to mimic the dominant ideology, and, at the same time, are driven by the desire to reassemble their broken history into a new organic relationship. People for whom faith is amphibolous are aware that such a restoration and rehabilitation are likely to be unattainable given the histories of failed attempts to establish a restored community by groups as Native Americans, Palestinians, as well as Asian Americans ourselves. Thus their expressions of faith, value, and perspective exist in a precarious state of being without any assurance of a glorious future. But those who embrace the amphibolous faith nevertheless *provisionally* insist and believe in "planting an apple tree even if the world comes to its end tomorrow." The amphibolous faith suggests that the alternative to an exclusive belief is not simply unbelief but a different kind of belief, one that embraces irresoluteness, disruption, and even

---

23. Said, *Huxley's Point Counter Point*.

uncertainty and yet enables the believer to respect that which we do not understand. In a complex world, wisdom is knowing that one does not really know for certain so that the believer can keep the future open with a provisional stance of faith as the *only* guide. The pathos of amphibolous faith indelibly etches its mark on the life and languages and voices of disfranchised people of America. The person of amphibolous faith longs, most of all, for a bridge-building amidst disrupted and estranged relationships, a bridge-building whose real meaning is an "interpretation of the worlds" through the grammar of amphiboly.

A new peoplehood may have a chance to be born in the world where another language is readily spoken, a language that welcomes amphibolous faith where eluding certainty has its value, as that which propels us into action, especially in those contexts where exploitation of those who are at the underside of life is palpable. From this responsible reaction to challenge the diminishment of fellow human beings, it is not difficult to perceive that amphiboly has its place. What is now needed is the commitment to allow our imaginations to work on transforming our heart, mind and soul, informing our lips and hands, inspiring our thoughts and actions so that amphibolous faith is recognized and valued for what it offers—that when we think we have grasped reality, whatever our intentions be, the reality passes through our minds, in front of us, eludes us and goes on its way. The future of peoplehood may well be a gathering of all people who are on the way together.

Bibliography

Adorno, Theodor. *Minima Moralia: Reflections from Damaged Life.* Translated by E. F. N. Jephcott. London: New Left, 1974.
Alhstrom, Sydney. *Religious History of the American People.* New Haven, CT: Yale University Press, 1974.
Althusser, Louis. *For Marx.* Translated by Ben Brewster. London: Verso, 1990.
Bhabha, Homi K. "Frontlines/Borderposts." In *Displacements: Cultural Identities in Questions,* edited by Angelika Bammer, 269–72. Bloomington: Indiana University Press, 1994.
———. *The Location of Culture.* London: Routledge, 1994.
Bellah, Robert N. *The Broken Covenant: American Civil Religion In Time of Trial.* Chicago, University of Chicago Press, 1992.
Bellah, Robert N., et al. *Habits of the Heart: Individualism and Commitment in American Life.* Berkeley: University of California Press, 1985.
———. "Is There a Common American Culture?" *JAAR* 66.3 (1998) 617–23.
Bercovitch, Sacvan. *The Puritan Origins of the American Self.* New Haven, CT: Yale University Press, 1975.
bin Talal, Hassan. Quoted in "Can Democracy Take Root in the Islamic World?: Seeing Iraq's Future By Looking at Its Past." *The New York Times* (July 18, 2003).
Brock, Rita Nakashima. "Response-Clearing Tangled Vines." *AJ* 22.1 (1996) 189–90.
Bulosan, Carlos. *America Is in the Heart: A Personal History.* Seattle: University of Washington Press, 1973.
Busto, Rudy. "Disorienting Subjects: Reclaiming Pacific Islander/Asian American Religons." In *Revealing the Sacred In Asian & Pacific America,* edited by Jane Naomi Iwamura and Paul Spickard, 9–28. New York: Routledge, 2003.
———. "The Gospel according to the Model Minority?: Hazarding an Interpretation of Evangelical College Students." *Amerasia Journal* 22 (Spring 1996) 133–47.
———. "The Predicament of Neplanta: Chicana(o) Religions in the Twenty-First Century," *Perspectivas* 1:1 (1998) 7–21.
Cha, Theresa Hak Kyung. *Dictee.* New York: Tanam, 1982.
Chen, Carolyn. "Cultivating Acceptance by Cultivating Merit: The Public Engagement of a Chinese Buddhist Temple in American Society." In *Revealing the Sacred: In Asian & Pacific America,* edited by Jane Naomi Iwamura and Paul Spickard, 80–84. New York: Routledge, 2003.

Chang, Soo-Chul, Hyun-Sook Kim, and Sook-Ja Chung. "Korean Woman Jesus: Drama Worship." Translated by Sook-Ja Chung. In *Mapping A Pan-Pacific Feminist Theology. The Journal of Women and Religion* 13 (1995) 45–50.

Cherlin, Andrew J. "Am O.k., You're Selfish." *New York Times Magazine* (October 17, 1999) 44–45.

Derrida, Jacques. "Force of Law." In *Deconstruction and the Possibility of Justice*, edited by Drucilla Cornell et al., 24–26. New York: Routledge, 1992.

———. *La Religion*. Edited with Gianni Vattimo. Paris: Seuil, 1996.

Drucilla Cornell, Michel Rosenfeld, David Gray Carlson, editors. *Deconstruction and the Possibility of Justice*. Routledge, 1992.

Doi, Joanne. "Bridge to Compassion: Theological Pilgrimage to Tule Lake an Manzanar." PhD diss., Graduate Theological Union, 2007.

———. "Tule Lake Pilgrimage: Dissonant Memories, Sacred Journey." PhD Comprehensive Exam, Graduate Theological Union, 2003.

Douglas, Mary. *Purity and Danger: An Analysis of the Concepts of Pollution and Taboo*. London: Routledge, 1966.

Espiritu, Yen Le. *Asian American Panethnicity: Bridging Institutions and Identities*. Philadelphia: Temple University Press, 1992.

———. *Asian American Women and Men: Labor, Laws, and Love*. Thousand Oaks, CA: Sage, 1997.

Du Bois, W. E. B. *The Souls of Black Folk*. New York: Simon & Schuster, 2005.

Fanon, Franz. *Black Skin, White Masks*. New York: Grove, 1967.

Faure, Bernard. *Chan Insights and Oversights: An Epistemological Critique of the Chan Tradition*. Princeton, NJ: Princeton University Press, 1993.

Fong, J. Craig. Quoted by Carlos Mendez in "A Fighter for Gay Rights." In *Asian Americans: Experiences and Perspectives*, edited by Timothy P. Fong and H. Shinagawa, 357–358. Upper Saddle River, NJ: Prentice Hall, 1999.

Gotanda, Neil. "Towards Repeal of Asian Exclusion," and "Our Constitution Is Colorblind." In *SLR* 44.1 (1991) 12–16.

Greider, William. *Who Will Tell the People: The Betrayal of American Democracy*. New York: Touchstone, 1993.

Groff, Warren F. *Christ the Hope of the Future: Signals of Promised Humanity*. Grand Rapids, MI: Eerdmans, 1971.

Hall, Douglas John. *Lighten the Darkness: Towards an Indigenous Theology of the Cross*. Rev. ed. Lima, OH: Academic Renewal, 2001.

Hall, Stuart. "Cultural Identity and Diaspora." In *Identity: Community, Culture, Difference*, edited by Jonathan Rutherford, 9–27. London: Lawrence and Wishart, 1990.

———. "New Ethnicities." In *Stuart Hall: Critical Dialogues in Cultural Studies (Comedia)*, edited by Kuan-Hsing Chen and David Morley, 441–449. New York: Routledge, 1996.

———. "Signification, Representation, Ideology: Althuser and the Post-Structuralist Debates." *Critical Studies in Mass Communication* 2.2 (1985) 91–114.

Hammond, Phillip E. *With Liberty for All: Freedom of Religion in the United States*. Louisville, KY: Westminster John Knox, 1998.

Holland, Joe. "The Capitalistic Threat." *The Atlantic Monthly* 279:2 (1997) 45–58.

———. *Faith And Culture: Historic Movement For The Catholic Laity*. South Orange: The Warwick Institute, 1988.

Holland, John, editor. *American and Catholic: The New Debate*. New York: Pillar, 1988.

Iwamura, Jane Naomi. "Critical Faith: Japanese Americans and the Birth of a New Civil Religion." No pages. Online: http://www.muse.jhu.edu. 2007.
Iwamura, Jane Naomi, and Paul Spickard, editors. *Revealing the Sacred in Asian & Pacific America*. New York: Routledge, 2003.
Jeung, Russell. *Faithful Generations: Faith and New Asian American Churches*. New York: Rutgers University Press, 2004.
———. "New Asian American Chruches and Symbolic Racial Identity." In *Revealing the Sacred: In Asian & Pacific America*, edited by Jane Naomi Iwamura and Paul Spickard, 241–71. New York: Routledge, 2003.
Jin, Ha. *War Trash*. New York, NY: Pantheon, 2004.
Johanssen, Robert W. Unpublished address at University of Illinois at Urbana-Champaign, 1998.
Kam, Kathrine. "False and Shattered Peace." In *California Tomorrow*. No pages. Online: http://www.californiatomorrow.org. 1989.
Kang, Younghill. *East Goes West*. New York, NY: Charles Scribner's Sons, 1937.
Kennerman, Barbara. "America's Best Leaders 2009." *US News and World Report* (November 4, 2009) 11–12.
Kim, David Kyuman. "Enchanting Diasporas, Asian Americans, and the Passionate Attachment of Race." In *Revealing the Sacred: In Asian & Pacific America*, edited by Jane Naomi Iwamura and Paul Spickard, 327–40. New York: Routledge, 2003.
Kim, Elaine H. "'Bad Women': Asian American Visual Artists Hahn Thi Pham, Hung Liu, and Yong Soon Min." In *Making More Waves: New Writing by Asian American Women*, by Elaine H. Kim, et al., 191–94. Boston: Beacon, 1997
———. "Room Viewed From a marginal Site: Texts, Contexts, and Asian American Studies." *JAAC* 1.2 (1994) 3–7.
Kim, Elaine, and Chungmoo Choi, editors. *Dangerous Women: Gender and Korean Nationalism*. New York: Routledge, 1997.
Koch, Adrienne, and William Peden, editors. *The Selected Writings of John and John Quincy Adams*. New York: Knopf, 1946.
Kingston, Maxine Hong. *The Woman Worrier*. New York: Vintage, 1977.
Kleine, Critiana. *Cold War Orientalism: Asia in the Middlebrow Imagination, 1945–1961*. Berkeley: University of California Press, 2003.
Kochiyama, Yuri. *Passing It On: A Memoir*. Edited by Marjorie Lee, Akemi Kochiyama-Sardinha, and Audee Kochiyama-Holman. Los Angeles: UCLA Asian American Studies Center Press, 2004.
Kogawa, Joy. *Obasan*. Boston, MA: David R. Godine, 1982.
Kramer, Paul. *The Blood of Government: Racial Politics in the American Colonial Philippines*. Baltimore: Johns Hopkins University Press, 2003.
Lane, Belden C. *Landscapes of the Sacred: Geography and Narrative in American Spirituality*. Isaac Hecker Studies in Religion and American Culture. New York: Paulist, 1988.
Lavie, Smadar, and Ted Swedenburg. "Introduction: Displacement, Diaspora, and Geographies of Identity." In *Displacement, Diaspora, and Geographies of Identity*, edited by Smadar Lavie and Ted Swendenburg, 1–25. Durham, NC: Duke University Press, 1991.
Lee, Marjorie, Audee Kochiyama-Holman, and Akemi Kochiyama-Sardinha, editors. *Passing It On: A Memoir*. Los Angeles: UCLA Asian American Studies Center Press, 2004.

Lee, Sang Hyun. "Pilgrimage and Home in the Wilderness of Marginality: Symbols and Contexts in Asian American Theology." *AJT* 7 (1993) 244–53.
Liu, Eric. *The Accidental Asian: Notes of a Native Speaker.* New York: Vintage, 1999.
Lincoln, Bruce. *Discourse and the Construction of Society: Comparative Studies of Myth, Ritual, and Classification.* Oxford: Oxford University Press, 1989.
Long, Charles H. *Significations: Signs, Symbols, and Images in the Interpretation of Religion.* Philadelphia: Fortress, 1986.
Lowe, Lisa. *Immigrant Acts: On Asian American Cultural Politics.* Durham, NC: Duke University Press, 1996.
Lukacs, Georg. *Theory of the Novel: A Historico-Political Essay on the Forms of Great Epic Literature.* Translated by Anna Bostock. Cambridge, MA: The MIT Press, 1993.
Lyotard, Jean-Francois. *The Differend: Phrases in Dispute.* Theory and History of Literature 46. Minneapolis: University of Minnesota Press, 1988.
Marty, Martin E. *Religion and Republic: American Circumstance.* Boston: Beacon, 1987.
Melville, Herman. *Moby Dick.* New York, NY: Oxford University Press, 2008.
Mirikitani, Janice. "Breaking Tradition" In *Shedding Silence: Poetry and Prose.* Berkeley, CA: Celestial Arts, 1987.
Morley, David, and Kuan-Hsing Chen, editors. *Stuart Hall. Critical Dialogues in Cultural Studies.* Comedia. London: Routledge, 1996.
Neuhaus, Richard John. "Farewell to the Overclass" In *RPL* 65 (1996) 81–86.
———. *The Naked Public Square: Religion and Democracy in America.* Grand Rapids, MI: Eerdmans, 1986.
Ng, David, editor. *People on the Way: Asian North Americans Discovering Christ, Culture, and Community.* Valley Forge, PA: Judson, 1996.
Niebuhr, H. Richard. *Christ and Culture.* New York: Harper, 1951.
———. *The Kingdom of God in America.* Hamden, CT: Shoe String, 1935.
———. *The Meaning of Revelation.* New York: Macmillan, 1962.
———. *Radical Monotheism and Western Culture.* New York: Harper, 1960.
———. *The Responsible Self: An Essay in Christian Moral Philosophy.* New York: Harper & Row, 1963.
Nietzsche, Friedrich. *On the Genealogy of Moral.* Translated by Walter Kaufmann and R. J. Hollingdale. New York: Vintage, 1969.
Nishikawa, Lane. "Grandfather." *Bridge* 4.4 (1976) 54.
Obama, Barak. "A More Perfect Union." *New York Times* (March 18, 2008) http://nytimes.com/2008/03/18/us/politics/18text-obama.html.
Oh, Angela E. *Open: One Woman's Journey.* Los Angeles: UCLA Asian American Studies Center Press, 2002.
Okado, Mitsuho. "A Challenge of Re-forming a Community in a Case of a Japanese American Church." DMin project, Pacific School of Religion, 2005.
Okihiro, Gary Y. "Is Yellow Black or White?" In *Asian Americans: Experiences and Perspectives,* edited by Timothy P. Fong and Larry H. Shinagawa, 63–78. New York: Prentice Hall, 2000.
———. *Margins and Mainstreams: Asians in American History and Culture.* Seattle: University of Washington Press, 1994.
———. "Religion and Resistance in America's Concentration Camps." In *Phylon: Review of Race and Culture* 45:3 (1984) 220–233.
Omi, Michael, and Howard Winant. *Racial Formation in the United States: From the 1960s to the 1990s.* 2nd ed. New York: Routledge, 1994.

Palumbo-Liu, David. *Asian/American: Historical Crossings of Racial Frontier*. Stanford, CA: Stanford University Press, 1999.

Putnam, Robert. "E Pluribus Unum: Diversity and Community in the Twenty-first Century." *Christian Science Monitor* (June 29, 2007) www.csmonitor.com/2007/0629/p08s01-comv.html.

Radhakrishnan, Rajagopolan. *Diasporic Mediations: Between Home and Location*. Minneapolis: University of Minnesota Press, 1996.

Rieff, David. "Their Hearts And Minds? Why the ideological battle against Islamists is nothing like the struggle against communism." *The New York Times Magazine* (September 4, 2004) 11–12.

Roak, James L. *Master without Slaves: Southern Planters in the Civil War and Reconstruction*. New York: Norton, 1977.

Rosenberg, Emily S. *Spreading the American Dream: American Economic and Cultural Expansion, 1890–1942*. American Century Series. New York: Hill and Wang, 1982.

Said, Edward W. *Culture and Imperialism*. New York: Vintage, 1994.

———. "Huxley's Point Counter Point Celebrates 75th Anniversary." Center for Book Culture.org (May 2003) No pages. Online: http://everything.explained.at/counterpoint.

———. "An Exchange: *Exodus and Revolution*." *Grand Street* 5 (1986) 246–59.

———. *Orientalism*. New York: Pantheon, 1978.

———. "Reflections on Exile." In *Out There: Marginalization and Contemporary Cultures*, edited by Russell Fergusson, Martha Gever et al., 357–68. Documentary Sources in Contemporary Art 4. Cambridge, MA: The MIT Press, 1990.

———. *Reflections on Exile and Other Essays*. Cambridge: Harvard Univerisity Press, 2002.

Santayana, George. *Scepticism And Animal Faith: Introduction To A System Of Philosophy*. New York: Dover, 1955.

Semaan, George. Quoted in James M. Wall, "Eyes to See, Ears to Hear." *CC* 118:26 (September 26, 2001) 45.

Singh, Jaideep. "9/11 & 7/7: A Cross-Atlantic Comparison of the Rising Tides of White and Christian Supremacy in the Wake of Terrorist Attacks." An unpublished manuscript, Pacific School of Religion, March 9, 2006.

———. "Sikhs and 9/11: Five Years Forward, a Hundred Years Back." An unpublished article, Pacific School of Religion, 2006.

Smith, Houston. Quoted in *Moyers On America: A Journalist and His Times*, by Bill Moyers, 74. New York: Anchors, 2004.

Smith, Jonathan Z. *Map Is Not Territory*. Chicago: The University of Chicago Press, 1978.

———. *To Take Place: Toward Theory in Ritual*. Chicago: The University of Chicago Press,1987.

Smith, Linda Tuhiwai. *Decolonizing Methodologies: Research and Indigenous Peoples*. Dunedin, NZ: University of Otago Press, 1999.

Sojourners in Asian-American and Biblical History. Vol 5: *Adult*. Asian-American Christian Education Curriculum Project. San Francisco: Golden Gate Mission Area, Synod of the Pacific, 1979.

Sobredo, James, Dennis O. Flynn, and Arturo Giraldez, editors *Studies in Pacific History: Economics, Politics, and Migration*. Burlington, VT: Ashgate, 2002.

Soros, George. "The Capitalist Threat." *The Atlantic Monthly* 279:2 (1997) 45–58.

Takagi, Dana Y. "Maiden Voyage: Excursion into Sexuality and Identity Politics in Asian America." *AJ* 21:1 (1994) 1–17.

Takaki, Ronald. *A Different Mirror: A History of Multicultural America*. Boston: Back Bay Book, 1994.

———. *A Larger Memory: A History of Our Diversity, with Voices*. Boston: Little, Brown, 1998.

Taylor, Charles. *A Secular Age*. Cambridge, MA: Belknap, 2007.

Tolstoy, Leo. *My Confession: And, The Spirit Of Christ's Teaching*. New York: T. Y. Crowell, 1887.

Turner, Victor. "Body, Brain, and Culture." *Zygon* 18 (September 1983) 21–25.

———. *The Ritual Process: Structure and Anti-Structure*. Lewis Henry Morgan Lectures. New York: Aldine, 1995.

Tocqueville, Alexis de. *Democracy in America*. Translated by George Lawrence. New York: Perennial Classics, 2000.

Uchida, Yoshiko. *Picture Bride*. Flagstaff, AZ: Northland Press, 1987.

Valentin, Benjamin. Editor. *New Horizons in Hispanic/Latino(a) Theology*. Cleveland: Pilgrim, 2003.

Wang, Lin Chi. "White Supremacy and the Bible." Presentation at Pacific School of Religion, October 8, 2004.

West, Cornel. *Democracy Matters: Winning the Fight Against Imperialism*. New York: Penguin, 2004.

Williams, Patrick, and Laura Chrisman, editors. *Colonial Discourse and Post-Colonial Theory: A Reader*. New York: Columbia University Press, 1994.

Wong, Nellie. *Dreams in Harrison Railroad Park: Poems*. Berkeley: Kelsey Street, 1977.

Wuthnow, Robert. *Religious Diversity: America and the Challenges of Religious Diversity*. Princeton, NJ: Princeton University Press, 2007.

Yoo, David K., editor. *New Spiritual Homes: Religion and Asian Americans*. Honolulu: University of Hawaii Press, 1999.

Yoo, David K., and Ruth H. Chung, editors. *Religion and Spirituality in Korean America*. Bloomington: University of Illinois Press, 2008.

Yoon, Jin-me. Quoted by Elaine Kim in "Room Viewed From a Marginal Site: Texts, Contexts, and Asian American Studies." *JAAC* 1.2 (1994) 5.

Yu, Henry. *Thinking Orientals: Migration, Contact, and Exoticism in Modern America*. Oxford, UK: Oxford University Press, 2001.

www.ingramcontent.com/pod-product-compliance
Lightning Source LLC
Chambersburg PA
CBHW070911160426
43193CB00011B/1430